CITIZEN

OF THE

WORLD

A Memoir

by Ernesto Flores
as told to Lynda Jones

ISBN: 979-8-5108057-6-5

To the hardworking people of Mexico, who made this story possible.

PART 1

• • •

Angels and Heroes

1

A Citizen of the World

Mazatlán, Mexico
1965

I was five years old when I became a citizen of the world. Before that, I was a menace. My whole life changed the day I started kindergarten.

My older brothers, Pedro and Pablo, went to kindergarten before me. Now Pablo was in elementary school and Pedro in *secondaria*. They wore uniforms every day to school. Tan pants and white shirts. Hard black shoes on their feet. Hair cut short and straight. Being in kindergarten, I was able to go to school in my shorts and a T-shirt, with my feet comfortable in huaraches and my hair left long and curly, the way I liked it.

My brothers told me that school was fun. That I would learn to read and do numbers. I wanted to go to school. I liked learning new things and making new friends. What my brothers didn't tell me about school was that I had to be quiet. I had to sit in my seat. I had to raise my hand to pee. I couldn't go out-side or even look out the window. I couldn't fight.

The night before I started kindergarten, my father said, "Neto, let's walk to the ocean. There's something I want you to know." Streetlights were already on as he took me outside, away from my brothers and sis-ters. Together, we walked along the dirt road in front of our house.

My father was a short man, shorter than my uncles, my mother's brothers. His arms and chest were broad and strong from swinging hammers in his black-smith shop by the downtown market. He wore long pants and T-shirts to work, so the skin on his arms was dark copper from the hot sun but his legs and his chest were almost white. I loved the way my fa-ther smelled as we walked together toward the beach. Man sweat mixed with tequila from a bottle kept on the top shelf in the corner of his shop.

"Ernesto," Papí told me, "I have always been proud of you. You are a happy, kind boy with a lot of energy. You are smart and a quick learner." My whole body smiled as I walked alongside my father and listened carefully to what he had to say.

"You are not like your brothers. They learn in school. But you, Neto, you learn from the world. You already know how to fix things and how to find your way home. Pablo and Pedro will tell you that you aren't as smart as they are, but they will never know as much as you do."

Papí stopped to light a cigarette and look up at the stars. I felt a soft, cool breeze coming from the ocean. As we reached the sand, I bent down to pick up a shell and put it in my pocket. It was an almost perfect shell, white with deep ridges down the front and shiny pink inside.

As we turned to go home, Papí bent down and put his hands on either side of my face. He looked me in my eyes. "But most of all, Neto, I want you to always remember that you are a good boy. Even if you make mistakes sometimes, you always try to do the right thing. Tomorrow, make sure your teacher knows that."

Mamí walked me to school that first day. The teacher walked me home. I don't remember my kindergarten teacher's name. I wasn't there long enough to learn it. I was there for only one day.

My mother didn't look happy when I walked into the house with the teacher beside me. The teacher didn't look happy either. A tall, skinny, dried-up woman, she shook her finger at my mother's face.

"Señora Flores, I cannot have your son, Ernesto, in my class. I won't let him come back to my school. I believe he is smart, but I cannot teach him."

Nobody was looking at me. I wanted to run, but I didn't know where to go. I stayed by the door, leaning against the wood, to hear what the teacher had to say.

"And the other students don't learn anything with Ernesto in class. He doesn't want to learn. He doesn't want to sit in his seat. All he wants to do is play and go outside."

"I'm sorry, Maestra. Ernesto is not like my other children. I don't know what to do with him."

"I suggest you send him to the military training school in Tepic. He needs discipline. He needs punishment. He needs to learn from the soldiers, not from a kindergarten teacher."

In 1965, it was not uncommon for families with a lot of children to send at least one of them away to school. Girls went to boarding school in Guadalajara. Boys, especially active boys from poor families, went to Internado Juan Escutia in Tepic, a reform school run by the army and paid for by the Department of Family Services.

Mamí decided at that very moment that the teacher was right. If I couldn't go to kindergarten, she didn't know what else to do with me. I was constantly sneaking out of the house. She didn't know where I was or when I would be home. But most of all, I threw things. I threw sticks, balls, rocks, toys, paper airplanes, anything that could fly.

For a long time, Mamí dreamed of me being in the army. She wanted me to have a career as a soldier, and my constant talk of wanting to be a pilot kept her dream alive. I drew simple pictures of the big silver planes I saw in the sky. I played with blocks of wood, pretending they were military planes. I wanted to fly a jet fighter over the ocean and bring it screaming in for a landing on a ship based near the Mazatlán harbor.

The day after the teacher brought me home, which should have been my second day of kindergarten but wasn't, Mamí told me she wanted to talk to me. "Neto, your father and I have decided that you and Pablo will go to school together in Tepic. You will be a military cadet at the Internado so you can learn to fly. Pablo is going so he can keep an eye on you."

One week later, there were four of us on the long bus trip to Tepic: my parents, my brother, and me. I didn't want to leave my little sisters or my baby brother. I didn't know what was going to happen to them or to me. I was able to say goodbye only because I knew that Pablo would be sitting next to me on the bus. We were going to be soldiers, together.

A tall, fat officer met us at the door of my new home. Much bigger than my father, he was a giant. He wore his whole military uniform, including his medals and his hat, which he took off as he shook my father's hand.

"Good morning, Mr. and Mrs. Flores. Thank you for bringing your boys to our school." My mother smiled at the officer and nodded her head.

"Please wait here while the boys are evaluated. This will take a few hours. We need to make sure your sons will be good cadets."

I didn't know that I needed to pass a test to go to school far away from home, but I did what I was told to do. I ran laps around the athletic field. I jumped over hurdles and climbed walls. I swung from ropes and walked across rocks. I did push-ups and jumping jacks. The tests were easy. These were things my friends and I did all the time back home.

When we finished testing, the sergeant asked my parents to sit down in front of his desk. Pablo and I were still standing as he closed the heavy wooden door.

"Mr. and Mrs. Flores, I am happy to tell you that Ernesto passed all the tests. He is strong and smart and athletic. He will be an excellent cadet. But," he continued, "I am sorry. Your other son, Pablo, failed. You need to take him back home with you. Pablo is not cut out to be in the military."

I didn't know what to think. *How could this happen?* I looked at my parents. My mother seemed happy. "Neto, you will stay here. This is the beginning of your military career." I tried to pay attention to her words, but they jumbled and roared in my ear.

"Pablo will come home with us and go back to Juan Carrasco Elementary School," she continued. My head was full of questions that I couldn't say.

"You can't come home with us, but we will visit you when we can."

My father had tears in his eyes as he said goodbye. He put his arms around me and pulled me close to him. Once again he said, "Neto, you are a good boy. Make sure the soldiers know that about you."

As I started to cry, he said, "Don't worry. You will be okay."

"But what about Pablo? And Rosa and Alicia? And Cachi?"

"They will be okay, too."

When I close my eyes, I still see my dormitory just as it was more than fifty years ago. Two long rows of bunk beds, fifteen bunks on each side of the cold cement room, with bars on two high windows. Sixty young cadets, ages five and six, too exhausted at the end of a day to even sigh.

My first night with the soldiers, alone in a room full of other boys, a guard came into the room and turned out the lights.

"Buenas noches, little cadets. Go to sleep. Be ready for tomorrow."

Suddenly, the room was as dark as the inside of a wolf's mouth, and I was afraid. I thought of my family going back to Mazatlán without me. *Maybe they've already forgotten about me,* I thought.

I said my prayers like Mamí always insisted. "*Padre nuestro que estás en los cielos* . . . Our Father, who art in Heaven . . ."

And in my ear, I heard my father whisper, as he always did, "*Buenas noches, m'hijo. Sueños con los angelitos.* Good night, my son. Sleep with the angels." I closed my eyes, and just as my father wished, sweet little angels surrounded me as I fell asleep.

2
Issi

Every day was the same. Little cadets, we got up in the dark at 5:30 a.m., with the Mexican anthem sounding like an eagle screaming in our ears. Sixty boys jumped out of warm beds and ran outside to get into straight lines, in groups of ten, under the glaring lights of the flagpole as the guards called out our names.

"Avila?"

"*Presente.*"

"Escodero?"

"*Presente.*"

"Flores?"

"*Presente.*"

"Gonzales?"

"*Presente.*"

The guards wanted to make sure that no one had run away overnight.

We pledged allegiance to the flag and exercised

outside in the cold morning air. Usually without trousers. Dressed only in our tennis shoes and underwear, we did calisthenics and sprinted around the huge, Olympic-sized athletic field. When we were tired and sweaty, we jogged to the showers to put on clean uniforms for the day. Crisp khaki pants and green T-shirts. Baseball caps on our freshly shaved heads. Army boots on our feet. After a hearty breakfast, we went to our classrooms for a full day of lessons.

In the beginning I was homesick, but I didn't know there was a word for what I felt. Sometimes, especially when I had to be quiet, I was afraid my eyes would start to water. I didn't want to eat, but Sargent Rudy told me I had to. Sitting in school all day, I did whatever the teacher told me to do. I remembered what my father said about being a good boy. I wanted to make him proud.

Issi and I discovered each other the first day we checked into the Internado. We were the same age, in the same dormitory. After breakfast, we went with Sergeant Rudy to the military store to get our uniforms. Next he marched us to the barbershop, a small space in a separate concrete building, away from the rest of the school. Issi and I looked at each other in the big barbershop mirror and decided we'd be friends.

Issi was embarrassed because he had a bad hair disease. He slid down in the chair and tried to cover his head with the towel. The barber took away the towel, turned on the clippers, and shaved his head bald. Issi started to cry as older boys laughed and pointed at him through the window.

"Look at that ugly little kid. His hair is falling out in big patches, just like a mangy dog. I don't want to be near him." And then they made barking noises, laughed, and poked each other in the ribs.

That first day, I woke up angry. I didn't want to talk to anyone. My family had left me, and now the barber was shaving off my long, curly hair. I pointed my chin to the ceiling and jerked my head around.

"Sit still or the clippers will cut your head. I don't want you to bleed all over my towel."

I crossed my arms in front of me and glared. It didn't matter. My curls fell in a brown pile on the white tile floor. My head was as bald as Issi's. *Who is that person?* I thought as I looked into the mirror. I wasn't going to cry.

• • •

From the beginning, Issi and I got in a lot of fights. Never with each other. Mostly with older kids. The fourth and fifth graders jumped us from behind and, before we knew it, we were fighting again. Kicking, punching, throwing people to the ground and stomping on them. Pounding them with our fists. Yelling and calling them names. Some fights we won and some we lost. We didn't care. It felt good to fight, to stick up for each other and for ourselves.

"Thanks, Neto, for jumping on that guy when he had me on the ground."

"No problem, Issi." He was my friend, and I would defend him no matter what.

Sargent Rudy knew about the fights, but he never punished us. "Listen. I love you guys," he said as he helped us get cleaned up. "You kids are going to make it."

When my father came to visit, Sargent Rudy found him and shook his hand. "Jesús, Ernesto is a good cadet. He will be a good soldier. He's loyal and willing to fight to help his friend. I'm glad he's here."

My father told me what Sargent Rudy said, and I knew I had made him proud. For the first time in my life, I'd made myself proud, too.

• • •

There were new cadets admitted to the school every week. I wondered how they felt. Were they afraid, lonely, and worried, just like me? Did they ever wake up and forget where they were? Did their hearts hurt, like mine, so that sometimes it was hard to breathe? I wanted to know who these new boys were.

"*Hola. Me llamo Neto. Como te llamas?* I am Ernesto. What is your name?"

"*Soy de Mazatlán?* I am from Mazatlán. Where are you from?"

"What position do you play in soccer?" I invited them to play on my team.

"Do you want to play during recess?" I told jokes and tried to make them smile.

"I am new here, too. My family left me because I wouldn't behave."

I asked them if they were lonesome for their families. Some, like Issi, were orphans from far away with no family to love. I told them not to be angry or they would get in trouble. Little by little, my life began to change. I made friends and I felt better.

There was no kindergarten at the military school, so I went straight to first grade. I liked school. I learned to read and add numbers. I learned things I never knew about before—interesting stories about Mexican people in history, facts about plants and animals. Sometimes I couldn't pay attention because I was thinking about my family and friends in Mazatlán. *Why was I such a troublemaker when I was living at home? What was wrong with me?*

When the teacher told us to take out a piece of paper and write our names, I always wrote my full name, Ernesto Alonso Flores Rodriguez, in big black letters. I was learning to write, and I didn't want to forget who I was.

3

Franco

I turned six years old in December and spent my birthday, Christmas, and Three Kings Day at the military school. By April, I had been with the soldiers for seven months. Some of my friends were going home for Easter vacation, and some of us would be staying at the military school. This was my first year, and I didn't know what was going to happen to me.

"Ven, *M'hijo. Vamanos!*" I heard my mother's voice. "*Vamos a Mazatlán para Semana Santa.*" I was going to Mazatlán for Easter vacation!

Never had my mother's voice sounded so good. I was going to spend two weeks at home with my family. I was so excited my heart thumped hard in my chest. I was going to see my little sisters, Alicia and Rosa. I would play soccer in the streets with my brother Pablo and my friends from the *colonia*. I would go to work in the blacksmith shop with Papí.

I would eat my mother's *sopa* and her chicken tamales. As I waved goodbye to the soldiers, I knew I was the luckiest boy in the world.

My cousins, Delia and Mercedes, were coming from their home in Hacienda del Tamarindo to help my mother get ready for Easter. I didn't know it right away, but they were also there to help my mother get ready for another baby. As we climbed on the big bus for the long trip from Tepic to Mazatlán, I noticed that my tiny mother was *gordita*. I was surprised to see that she was going to have another baby very soon. My parents already had six children, and Cachi wouldn't be two until October.

People were happy to see me when I got home. Some of the neighbors stopped me in the street to welcome me back. Lupe, from across the street, made a special cake for me and my family. Señor Valdez, who lived in the house next door, patted my back and told me he missed me. My brothers and sisters wanted me to play with them. My mother didn't fuss at me the way she used to. My father and I went for long walks after dinner and talked about my life at the military school.

I was home for a week when my father pulled me aside, late one night. The others were sound asleep, but I was still awake.

"Quick, Neto. Go find Hermán Vega and tell him that we need to take your mother to the hospital." My father's forehead was creased, and his words came out quickly. "Hermán needs to bring his bus. It's time for the baby to be born."

We didn't know anybody who owned a car. Most men rode bicycles everywhere they went, but Hermán Vega drove a big Mazatlán bus. He and my father had been friends for a long time. They worked together at Camioneros Unidos, the bus driver's union, where Hermán was a driver and my father worked part time as a mechanic.

I have always been a very fast runner. My legs are long and strong, and I like to run. Rain drummed on the sidewalks and settled the dust on the dark street as I raced to find Papi's compadre. I listened to the sound of my feet splashing in the rain. My wet T-shirt was starting to stick to my back as I beat on Señor Vega's door.

Hermán answered the door wearing a stretched-out white T-shirt and tan baggy pants. His white hair stood straight up, wild in all directions. His sleepy eyes opened wide when he saw me. He took a step backward, then smiled and laughed out loud.

"Well, Neto, look at you, pounding on my door this late at night."

"Señor Vega, I need you to bring your big bus to my house. You have to hurry. My mother is going to have a baby and we need to get her to the hospital right away."

I ran all the way back home. I was not even out of breath when Hermán parked his bus in front of our house. Now he was wearing his brown bus driver's shirt and had a baseball cap on his head to cover his messy, white hair.

Papí stood before the picture of the Virgin of Guadalupe, silently praying to her for help.

Hermán's long arm circled my father's shoulders. "Don't worry, Jesús. Zelmira is going to be okay."

My father shook his head. "We must hurry, amigo. She is in a lot of pain. I think this baby is coming too soon."

My father picked up my mother, carried her onto the bus, and laid her down on a mat on the floor. I had never seen or heard anything like this before. My mother screamed like an animal caught in a trap. She groaned and held her stomach. Her pinched face was an angry red. Her thick black hair was wet from sweat. Thunder, like cannon fire, rumbled in the distance. Lightning flashed in front of the bus, lighting our way to the hospital.

Mamí squeezed my father's hand as hard as she could. He talked to her in his most quiet voice. "Please, Zelmira, hold on. Keep breathing. We can't have this baby on the bus. Just a few more minutes, Mamí. Just a few more minutes. Hermán's bus will get us there in time."

The bus bounced and rattled as it raced through the streets of Mazatlán with my father, my mother, and me inside. It was a little past midnight when we arrived, the rain heavier than before.

"We'll go to the emergency door," Hermán shouted. "Once Zelmira is in the hospital, I'll leave my bus under the streetlight while we wait outside."

• • •

I often wonder why I was the only child allowed to ride with my parents on the bus from our house to the hospital. I think it was because I was closer to my father than any of the others. Papí knew that even though I was only six, I could be in charge and do whatever he told me to do. I was quick and strong. I could take care of myself.

Or maybe it was because the last time Delia came to help my mother, I swore at her and called her *"puta"* and *"pinche* Delia." She always laughed when I called her names, but my mother didn't think Delia was strict enough with me. For whatever reason, I was there when Franco was almost born on Hermán's bus. I saw and heard the whole thing.

"The baby's coming. It's coming right now," my mother screamed as the bus pulled in front of the hospital.

My father leaped off the bus onto the curb and ran inside Sanatorio Mazatlán to find a nun. In less than a minute, Sister Veronica climbed on the bus, wrapped a blanket around my mother's shoulders, and steered her down the steps and into the hospital. My father ran to open the door. He kissed the top of my mother's head as she entered the hospital. "I'm sorry, Mamí. I love you. Thank you. Thank you. Thank you for going through this again."

My father, Hermán, and I waited outside the hospital, under the cover of a big leafy mango tree, trying to stay out of the steady, cold rain. We smelled the sweet perfume of the last remaining blossoms of spring. Everything was quiet. There was no traffic on the street. Even the community dogs were sheltered for the night. Papí and Hermán took deep breathes as they inhaled their cigarettes. I was excited to be with them, out late in the rain, waiting for the nurse to come outside with her big, black umbrella and the news that my brother Franco was born.

"Congratulations, Señor Flores. You have another baby boy."

"Gracias, Hermana. How is Zelmira?'

"She is fine. She's sleeping now. You can come back tomorrow to see her and the baby."

Papí and Hermán were joking and laughing as we crossed the street, climbed back on the bus, and rode home along the quiet, wet streets of Mazatlán.

People told me that Franco looked just like me. As we got older, I realized that it was true and that it was not such a good thing.

That was the last time my mother gave birth. Mamí's battle to raise all of us had begun.

In one year, I saw a boy born and another boy die. It was life and death on the streets of Mazatlán.

4
Emilio

I've seen a lot of people die in my lifetime. Sometimes I wonder why I wasn't one of them. I've seen people drown, and once I saw a judge assassinated by gangsters right in front of my eyes. But nothing compares to when my friend Emilio died without warning when I was five.

The day started the same as any other day. The morning was quiet as we hurried out of our houses without saying a word to the people inside. Pelicans flew over the ocean, crisscrossing a perfect, cloudless blue sky. Soft breezes fanned palm trees, gently moving dust across the road. Along the ocean, buses lurched and ground their gears, picking up men and women going to work. Up and down the street, rooftop dogs barked warnings that we couldn't understand. Far in the distance, up against the mountains, was a hint of dark clouds and danger.

Emilio and Güero were cousins who lived with

their grandmother, Virginia Canedo, across the street from me. Emilio was four years old, and Güero was six. Güero's real name was José Luis, but everyone called him Güero because his skin was so light. We were good friends who, more than anything, loved playing in the street. We liked climbing on a big black truck that was used for hauling construction materials. The truck belonged to a friend of my father, who parked it overnight on the street where we lived.

The day of the accident, Emilio, Güero, and I were on top of the truck, laughing and throwing a little red ball. The ball bounced into the street, and Emilio and I scrambled down to get it. Güero stayed on top of the truck.

Emilio got to the ball first and threw it in front of the truck, where I was standing. I caught the ball, and Emilio ran over to meet me. We both started to climb back into the truck, but I got in first. Emilio was trying to climb in, when a taxi driver came screaming around the corner. Emilio was knocked to the ground, and the taxi driver ran over him. I jumped off the truck to see what happened, but my friend was already dead. One minute we were alive and laughing, and the next minute Emilio was dead.

Virginia Canedo heard the taxi squeal and then speed away. She ran out of her house, screaming and crying, but there was nothing anyone could do. She picked up Emilio's dead body and held him like a baby. My parents ran out into the street. They wrapped their arms around Señora Canedo and Emilio. Papí ran back to our house to get a chair.

"Here, Virginia. Please sit down."

My brothers saw what happened and started yelling at me and Güero. Until then, no one noticed us standing on top of the truck, the red ball still in my hands.

"Why did you let this happen?" my brothers wanted to know. "This is your fault. Why were you playing on the truck?"

I've asked myself that same question a thousand times since that day.

Something happened to both me and Güero the day Emilio died. From then on, Güero and I became good friends because we were always thinking of Emilio. Even if we didn't say anything about what happened that day in the street, we knew what the other person was thinking. In some ways, we each became tougher and more reckless from that day on. I believe that Emilio's spirit was always with us, even though he was dead.

Later that year, Güero left his grandmother's house and went to live with his parents in Cúliacan, and I was on my way to the military school. We were in middle school when Güero came back to Mazatlán and lived with his grandmother again. By that time, I was back from Tepic, and my family had moved to a different house, in a different *colonia*.

Güero and I went to separate schools, but we still

connected often until I left for the United States. As teenagers, Güero liked to ride motorcycles, and I went out to meet the ocean on my surfboard.

My friend Güero died in 1989 in a horrible motorcycle accident, but I am still alive to tell the story of what happened a long time ago. Emilio's death was my first encounter with angels. Ever since then, angels have come like spirits into my life, saving me even when I didn't deserve to be saved.

5
Mamí

When I was four years old, I threw a bicycle spoke that landed in my mother's eye. She screamed and put her hand over the wound. My spoke made her blind in that eye forever. I still don't know why I threw the spoke. I didn't mean to hurt her. I loved my mother. I always will.

When my brothers saw what I had done, they chased me out of the house and beat me up. They pushed me down on the ground and started kicking me. I grabbed their ankles, wrestled them to the ground, and punched them back. As soon as I could, I jumped up out of the dirt and ran to Virginia Canedo's house across the street. I didn't knock on the door. I just ran straight inside the house without saying anything. Señora Canedo was my mother's friend and the grandmother of my best friends, Emilio and Güero.

"Neto, who did this to you?" Señora Canedo pressed her lips together and shook her head when she saw me. My shirt was torn and dirty. My face and hair were streaked with dust. My lip was swollen and bleeding.

"Quick, Neto, hide under the long tablecloth in the kitchen." My heart pounded as my brothers beat on her door, looking for me.

"Señora Canedo, we're looking for Neto. Is he here?"

"No, I haven't seen him. Go look somewhere else."

I stayed there until it was dark outside and the moon was starting to come up in the sky. I walked home, but I didn't eat anything. I went right to my room and laid on my bed and cried. My mother never forgave me for throwing that bicycle spoke in the living room.

From that day on, I couldn't do anything right. When I offered to help, my mother told me to go outside. If I wanted to play with my brothers and sisters, they said I was a monster. My skin turned ugly, like a dog's. Nobody needed me. Nobody wanted me around.

To this day, whenever I look at Mamí, with her one blind eye, I know I would gladly give her one of my eyes if only she would let me.

By 1969, I had been at the military school for almost four years. I never told anybody about the day I threw the bicycle spoke. I wanted to go home, but I was afraid of what I might do. My father came to visit me once in a while, when he wasn't working. I was always happy to see him and to talk to him about my life in Tepic. Papí understood me. But my mother always wanted me to be someone else. Someone I could never be.

I was nine years old the day my father took me out of the military school. We walked together up the path to our house. My mother was sweeping the evening dust from the sidewalk when she saw us coming toward her. She rushed at us, screaming insults, her straw broom raised over her head.

"It's okay, Neto. Mamí is surprised to see you, that's all." My father leaned toward me, his strong arms hugging me tightly to his chest. The broom crashed over our huddled bodies. My mother's black eyes blazed with fury.

"Take him back. Take him back right now!" Her face turned dark red as the words spit out of her mouth. Her eyes were as cold as wet cement.

Up and down the street, doors and windows opened to the sound of my mother's curses and the relentless pounding of her broom across my father's strong back. The whole neighborhood witnessed the horror of my homecoming.

When my mother was finally too tired to lift her weapon one more time, my father quietly took it from her hands and we walked into the house together.

"Mamí, I couldn't leave him there. When I went to visit, Neto didn't recognize me. He didn't know who I was." My father's voice was quiet and sad. "Our son didn't know my face or my voice. I couldn't walk away and leave him there. I was afraid of the kind of person he was becoming. I was afraid we would lose him forever."

"Why did the soldiers let you take him?"

"I told Sergeant we were going to get something to eat and go to a movie. I took him right to the bus station, instead. I never brought him back."

I've heard my mother retell this story a thousand times. She always ends the story the same way. "Your father should never have taken you out. You were going to have a career in the army. You were going to learn to fly. He ruined your life."

But I was happy to be home. Happy to be with my brothers and sisters. Happy to be in the *colonia* with my friends. Happy to be back on Papagayo Street and away from the soldiers forever.

6
Lady

I returned home from the military school and easily finished fourth grade at Primaria Independencia. Then I transferred to Juan Carrasco Elementary School for fifth and sixth grades. In Mexico, children go to public school either in the morning or in the afternoon. At the Internado, I was in the classroom for eight hours a day. Going to regular school was easy.

Summers were filled with all the things I loved most. I was free to play outside and walk on the dusty paths through my neighborhood. I left home in the morning and didn't come back until the church bells rang for dinner. North Beach was an easy ten-minute walk from my house. On quiet mornings, as I ate my breakfast, I could hear the ocean waves calling me to come and explore.

I always loved the ocean, the salty smell of the water and the feel of soft, shifting sand under my feet.

The steady pulse of the waves. The shimmer on the water as the sun rose in the clear Pacific sky. The laughing shrieks as children chased each other across the shore.

By 1970, Mazatlán had a reputation as an ideal vacation spot for swimming and sport fishing. Like me, tourists had discovered the joy of a laid-back lifestyle along the beautiful white beaches of my city. I had a lot in common with the people who came to Mexico to swim and fish and watch for the next wave to kiss the sand.

The summer before sixth grade, I walked to the beach every day on my travels around the neighborhood. One day I saw a grown man selling salty peanuts and sweet bubblegum. He looked tired and sad. His back was stiff as he bent over his tray of peanuts.

"What are you doing?" I asked. "You look tired. Do you need some help?"

The man looked up and saw me standing in front of him. "You are right. I am tired and I am old. I'm going to be here all day. Would you like to help me sell some peanuts?"

"I can do that." I smiled. "I am Ernesto. What should I do?"

"Thank you, Ernesto. I will fill these little cups with warm peanuts and put them on a tray for you. Each bag is five pesos. When the tray is empty, come back for more. At the end of the day, I will pay you for being my helper."

The vendor and I made a good team that summer. He toasted the peanuts on his grill and poured them into tiny paper cups. Twenty cups on my tray. He gave me a quick lesson on how to sell peanuts and how to speak English. I was happy to be a beach seller. It was my first paying job. A good job for a boy who was ten years old.

At first the only English phrase I knew was "Peanuts! Peanuts! I have peanuts for you!" Gradually I learned more words that I practiced until they became part of me. Every morning I set up my tray on a stand under a palm tree and watched for people to flag me down from the beach. Then I would pick up my tray and run across the hot sand. Most days I earned fifty cents. Once in a while, Señor would give me an American silver dollar to take home to my mother. I was happy to help my family. But mostly, I was happy to work with my new friend, the peanut vendor.

I liked being around the tourists. They were kind and generous. Their happy, healthy faces were a reflection of the ocean to me. They liked to tease me and make me smile. They treated me with tenderness that I had never felt before. The women, especially the American women, said they liked my dark brown, curly hair and soft hazel eyes. They called me *comico y lindo*, funny and cute. Sometimes they called me honey. They said they wanted to adopt me and take me back home with them. They loved my hustle and my sassy smile.

I remember the women who were especially kind to me. I think of one of them to this day. I called her Lady. Lady had long, wild, blond hair and painted toenails. She was tall with skin toasted from the sun. Every day, Lady walked across the street from the Agua Marina Hotel with her little, blond American baby boy snuggled in a carrier strapped to her chest. She wore a long white dress over her light blue bathing suit. She carried an umbrella and a straw basket filled with the things she would need on the beach—baby oil, extra diapers, a book to read, water, and snacks. I watched for Lady every day as I ran up and down the hot, dry sand. I think she watched for me, too.

"Good morning, Ernesto. *Cómo estas?* How are you?" Her words were like sweet Coca-Cola to me.

"*Estoy bien. Y tu?* I am fine. And you?"

"*Yo también.* I'm fine, too."

Some days Lady would let me sleep under her big umbrella on a blanket next to her baby, telling me, "I will sell your peanuts for you if you want to take a nap." Often, she would rock her baby in her arms and sing him to sleep. Her voice was soft and calm, the voice of an angel singing a lullaby to her son.

The sand felt cool under the shade of Lady's umbrella, and I would fall asleep quickly. When I woke up, Lady would laugh, show me the empty tray and give me a fistful of change. For years, I thought that she was the best peanut seller on the beach. Only after I was grown and moved away did I realize that Lady bought my entire tray of peanuts herself, while I was sleeping under the soft, comforting wings of her umbrella.

7

Abuelo

My grandfather, Pacho Rodriguez, chased my cousin
Prieto and me away from the river and down the
cobblestone streets of La Hacienda. Abuelo was on
horseback, flicking his leather horsewhip across our
bare backs. We ran naked in front of his horse, up
and down the familiar streets and alleys of La Hacienda, past the cement houses and open yards where
my relatives lived. Past the horses and mules and burros eating grass in their corrals. Past women feeding
chickens and children kicking soccer balls in front
of their homes. Everyone stopped to see what was
happening. Even the animals stopped chewing long
enough to look up. I was afraid Pacho was going to
kill us both. We were twelve years old.

My mother often took me and my sisters to La Hacienda del Tamarindo, the town where she was born
and where her family still lived. I loved riding the
big comfortable bus from Mazatlán to Rosario. I was

even more excited when we boarded the smaller local bus that took us rattling and burping our way over dirt roads, barely missing cows and goats grazing outside the bus, up to the entrance of La Hacienda.

As the bus finally shuddered and hissed to a stop, kicking up a cloud of dust, my cousin Prieto sprinted out his front door, crossed the courtyard in front of the church, made a quick sign of the cross, and met us at the town gate. From then on, until it was time for us to go back to Mazatlán, he and I were inseparable.

Prieto and I were born the same year and had the same grandfather. My grandmother, Maria Aguilar, was Pacho's first wife. When she died in 1932, Pacho married Beatrix Martinez, Prieto's grandmother. I called Prieto my cousin, but we were closer than brothers. I always stayed at Prieto's house and loved his mother, my Tia Olga, with all my heart.

On weekends and in the summer at La Hacienda, Prieto and I rode every available animal with four legs. Always bareback, we rode horses, mules, and donkeys. We hopped on the backs of the cows and rode the young bulls whenever we could catch them.

"Hey, Prieto, I have an idea." I announced one day. "I'm going to walk away from the corral, so the bull thinks I am going home. You tell me when he looks away. Then I'll run back, grab his horns, and hop on."

Prieto looked back at the young bull standing there, glaring at us. He grinned and cocked his head toward the bull. He took his hands out of his pockets, scratched his head, and wiped his hands on the front of his jeans.

"Good idea, Neto. I hope it works."

Most of the time the bulls were smarter than we were. But we were young *charros*. We didn't mind being thrown in the dirt.

Prieto and I were the same size. His real name was Felix, the same as my great-grandfather's. We called him Prieto because his skin was dark, much darker than mine. People say they can always tell Rodriguez men by the sparkle in our eyes and our quick, strong laugh. Prieto and I had both. His thick black hair was cut short, not left long and curly like mine. Although we were skinny kids back then, we were athletic and strong. We loved roaming the streets of La Hacienda, looking for something to do.

Pacho's name was a combination of *padre* and Nacho, the shortened version of Ignacio. It was a term of respect if not of endearment. To this day, everyone who knew him will tell you that Abuelo was a mean man. We didn't like him. I don't think anybody did. I know he didn't like children, and he certainly didn't like us.

Like most boys at that time, we were disciplined at home, but we rebelled against our grandfather whenever we were out of the house. I believe to this day that Pacho hated to see anyone, especially children, laughing and having fun. He was a dictator, a harsh ruler, an angry, hateful person. Although we tried to stay away from him, Prieto and I were usually the focus of his fury. Abuelo was a tyrant. He ordered us around as if we were his slaves. But we weren't his slaves. We were kids with a lot of energy. We wanted to play. We hated his rules and being told what to do.

Unlike Abuelo, his children—the men and women of La Hacienda—were sweet, gentle, hardworking people. They respected and honored their spouses and loved all the children of the village. Prieto and I liked to help them wherever we could. It was part of our boyish nature.

There were no wells or water pumps in La Hacienda in 1972. If Tia Valvina or Tia Olga needed water from the river, Prieto and I volunteered to bring a donkey and fetch water for her. We were happy to bring water to anyone else in town, too. We went from house to house, looking for work.

"*Buenos diás, señora.* How are you today? Do you need any fresh water from the river?"

"*Buenos diás, niños.* You are up early. Yes, I could use a jug of water. Thank you for stopping by."

It often took us all morning, making trips back and forth to Rio Baluarte to bring fresh, clean water to the women of La Hacienda. We loaded each burro with two empty ceramic water jugs, hopped on their broad backs, and rode to the river. The donkeys' gray hides bristled against our blue jeans as we plodded along the dirt road.

The water in Rio Baluarte was clean and cold coming from the sierra. The burros waited patiently in the shade as we filled each water jug, one by one, with twenty liters of cold water and strapped them to their backs. Slowly we led the burros into town, where we unloaded the heavy jugs for the housewives, who were happy to see us. The women praised us and told us what good boys we were. Sometimes they gave us a few pesos for our work. Then we started over again, leading the burros from house to house, strapping on a new batch of empty water containers, and returning to the river.

Prieto and I worked hard, going back and forth to the river. Sometimes we made as many as seven trips, each donkey carrying forty liters of clean water at a time. When we finished collecting water for the day, hot and tired and covered in dust, the donkeys smelled better than we did. We knew we were supposed to lead the burros back home, and often we did, but they knew the way home without us. Sometimes, after the last trip of the day, we gave their rumps a slap and told them to go home while we stayed and played in the river, jumping from rock to rock and swimming in the ice-cold water.

That's where we were the day I looked up and saw Abuelo in the distance, as silent and deadly as a devil's fart. He was an exceptionally large, light-skinned man, sitting tall on his great white horse. He wore a white, flat-brimmed sombrero that made him look even more frightening. Pacho looked like a phantom trotting down the road toward us.

"Quick, Prieto. Grab our clothes from the riverbank and run for the bushes," I yelled. "*Apurate! Hurry Up!*"

We tried to make it to the other side of the river, but it was too late. We hid behind a huge huancastle tree just as Pacho's horse started to gallop. He was on top of us before we had time to grab our clothes.

The veins on Abuelo's neck bulged purple. He shook his fist and raised his whip in the air. His eyes bored through us as he shouted, "I caught you, *cabrones*. You aren't going to get away this time. I've been looking for the two of you all over town."

Spit flew from his mouth as he pulled his horse up behind us. "You can't fool me, *pinche pendejos*. I knew I would find you here." He called our mothers names too terrible to put on this piece of paper. I don't think I had ever seen anyone that full of rage.

Prieto and I ran through bushes and over rocks. We ran eight hundred meters along the road without stopping. We ran across the square in front of the church, where cows were sleeping in the shade.

Abuelo chased us like he was chasing cattle. We didn't need to look back. We knew he was there by the thunder of his horse and the fury in his voice. Every turn we made, Abuelo was right behind us, yelling and flicking his switch. We ran, naked, all the way straight to Gero's and Valvina's house, where we knew we would be safe. It was our sanctuary. Tio Gero had thrown Abuelo out of the house a long time ago, and from then on Abuelo wasn't allowed to go inside.

We were breathless, our chests on fire, as we charged through the front door.

"*O, Dios mio,*" screamed Valvina. "Where are your clothes?"

Before we could answer, Valvina ran to the back of the house, to the laundry shed on the other side of the patio. She came back with two pairs of pants and two clean T-shirts that belonged to my cousin Jáime.

"Put these on. They are a little big, but they are fine for now," she said, shaking her head. "It's better than wearing nothing at all."

We were happy to have clothes on again. The cotton shirts felt good against our oozing, bloody backs. Valvina wrapped her arms around us and hugged us to her big soft chest. "*M'hijos,* when the burros came back without you, I knew where you were. Don't ever swim in the river again without permission." But she knew we would.

Valvina gave us each a glass of cold milk, some sweet bread, and fruit. Soon her house was full of neighbors asking us to tell them the story of how Abuelo chased us home.

My family still loves to tell the story of me and Prieto running naked for our lives on that hot summer day when we were twelve. We liked being celebrities, but after that day, Prieto and I hated our grandfather more than ever. We never again referred to him as anything other than Abuelo. We refused to call him Pacho. When he died in 1989, both of us told the story again. We toasted each other with a glass of tequila. And we laughed.

8

Memo

Men in my neighborhood rode their bicycles to work every day. I finished sixth grade in June and would be starting *secondaria* in September. I was certainly old enough to earn a bicycle. I needed a job.

The first person I asked for a job was Memo, the guard at the *panaderia* where my mother bought bread for our family. His full name was Guillermo Chavez. In the United States, he would be called Bill or Willy. In Mexico, his name was Memo.

"Do you need any help, Señor Chavez?" I asked. "I can sweep floors and do whatever you need." I smiled so hard my cheeks puffed out. Memo smiled back at me.

"Maybe I can use some help," suggested Memo. "Can you come in at night? I need someone to help me clean the bakery after the bakers leave."

"Sure," I answered. "I can do anything you need me to do." I looked around. Pieces of dough were stuck on the long, metal tables. Floors were dusted with flour. The smell of hot ovens and fresh bread was still in the air. I bounced from foot to foot as I thought of the bicycle that soon would be mine. I started work that same week, on a hot summer night when I was twelve years old.

La Flor de Mazatlán was one of the few *panaderias* in Mazatlán in 1972. It was two kilometers from my home in Colonia Lomas del Mar. The walk took me thirty minutes, and I came to love every meter of that journey. My heart sang with confidence as I thought of earning money and spending time with Memo in the quiet nights, as we got the bakery ready for another day. Memo was *chaparo*, short and strong. He was kind and patient as he taught me to use the cleaning tools and scrub all the equipment. More than anything, Memo watched out for me and wanted me to be safe. He didn't want me to get hurt.

The work was hard in the beginning, as Memo taught me the routine after the bakery shut down for the night. My first job was cleaning the aluminum blades of the bread mixers. Then I learned to use sharp spatulas to scrape dough off the tables. I used the broom and a mop to clean flour off the floors. Twice a week, I scrubbed the floors using a bucketful of soapy water and a hand brush. I made sure that I scoured every inch of the floor, including the corners, before dumping the dirty water into the street.

I worked from 8:00 p.m. until 2:00 a.m. five nights

a week, getting the bakery ready for the four bread bakers who came to work in the early hours of the morning. The clay ovens were fired and bread was baking by 3:00 a.m. The *panaderos* were magicians with bread dough. Sometimes their hands moved so fast I couldn't keep track of what they were doing. I loved the harsh slap of dough being pounded on long metal tables and the thump of hot bread falling out of their baking pans.

In addition to the four bread bakers, there were two cake bakers who came in twice a week to make beautiful cakes. They made fancy fiesta cakes for every occasion—weddings, *quincineras*, birthdays. Everyone wanted a cake from La Flor.

About the same time that I started working, my mother began selling groceries out of our house to earn extra money. After a couple of weeks, Memo asked me, "How would you like to take some bread home for your mother to sell? I can give it to you for half price." Mamí liked the idea right away. Nothing was better than a piece of bread from the bakery to go with our morning coffee. Pretty soon my mother was happily selling delicious, day-old bread to our neighbors, along with tomatoes, avocados, bananas, and fresh mangoes from the neighborhood market.

Soon there was no stopping her. Mamí greeted me as I walked in the door after work. She was in a hurry, on her way to the big market downtown. She rode the bus to Pino Suaréz Market and came home in a taxi with pineapples, apples, and guavas. She bought celery, carrots, onions, garlic, and chiles. Rice, potatoes, beans, milk, cheese, and eggs. Dozens and dozens of eggs.

My mother continued to buy day-old bread from Memo and enlarged the store in what had been our living room. She started taking orders from our neighbors, delivering meat and poultry to them for an extra charge.

Soon she was also cooking, making *tortas, molletes*, and juices to sell for breakfast. Our house became a neighborhood grocery store and a small restaurant. My mother was the storekeeper and the cook. My father didn't like what my mother was doing, but she was a woman with a mission and she was the boss. She was earning money for my oldest brother to go to college in Cúliacan.

One night Memo said he wanted to talk to me. I hoped I wasn't in trouble. He wrinkled his forehead so that his eyebrows came together in a single, straight line.

"Neto, I worry about you walking home late at night. The path is dark, and sometimes there aren't even stars or a moon to show you the way home."

Memo was worried that something would happen to me as I walked the thirty minutes to my house at two in the morning.

"I can make a bed for you in the corner of the bakery. You will be okay here until the sun comes up."

Memo made a bed for me on top of bags of flour, and I slept there most nights until it was time to go home. While I was sleeping, the bakers were busy making *bolillos, taleras,* and loaves of bread to load into delivery trucks at sunrise. The bakers singing along to the ever-present radio, and the smell of fresh coffee and bread right from the oven, was my alarm clock. As soon as the sun rose in the sky, I was on my way home, humming to myself as I listened to the cooing of *palomas* sitting on the telephone wires that stretched from pole to pole.

Summer was coming to an end, and soon it would be time to go back to school. *No problema!* I brought my uniform and shoes to the bakery. I worked for six hours, then slept on my flour-sack bed until it was time to change into my clean white shirt, blue pants, and hard black shoes and walk to school.

After working with Memo for two and a half months, I saved enough money to put a down payment on my bicycle. The seller let me take the bike because I agreed to make payments to him. Every week I went to find him and give him my money.

My bike was called a *chicharroneras.* It was the kind of bicycle used by street-sellers who sold *chicharones*—crispy, fried pork skins—throughout the city. It was a heavy-duty bike, made mostly of iron and painted brown. By Christmas I had paid it all off. It was mine.

My new bicycle was so tall I had to stand on the

sidewalk to reach the pedals. I leaned the bike away from the curb and pushed down on the pedals with my tiptoes to start the bike in motion. After a week, I figured out how to lower the seat to fit the length of my legs. I knew I was growing taller when I didn't need the sidewalk anymore.

I made a cage for the back of the bike, to hold the bread that I took home every morning to my mother. With my new bike, the ride to the bakery took five minutes. I felt like I was flying. I no longer needed to walk to school from the bakery. I had time to ride home, deliver bread to my mother, change into my school uniform, and still be on time for school.

Riding home after my night shift at the bakery, I smiled and said hello to the men from my neighborhood, who were riding their bikes to work for the day. They smiled and greeted me with nods of their heads as we passed each other on the street.

I rode that bike everywhere for the next three years, until I started surfing and didn't need it anymore. I couldn't carry my surfboard and pedal at the same time, so I went back to walking. I gave the bike to my dad, and he rode it to work for many years.

I stayed with Memo and worked five shifts a week until the end of the first semester, eight months total. Memo covered my shifts on weekends so I could play soccer and do my homework, but my mother started to fuss at me. She didn't like me working after school started. She wanted me to be a good student, and she was afraid that if I kept working, I would quit school. Mamí thought I couldn't keep working nights and be ready for school at seven in the morning. I still think I could have done it. I loved school as much as I loved working at the bakery. I stopped working full time at Flor de Mazatlán in January, soon after I turned thirteen.

Memo didn't want me to leave the *panaderia*, but my mother insisted she didn't need my money, and my bicycle was paid for. I never wanted to leave Don Memo. I loved him and he was an excellent sponsor. He taught me much more than how to safely clean bakery equipment. He taught me to work for what I wanted. He taught me to be proud of a job well done. Along with my dad, Memo taught me to be a man.

9

Nolas

Mazatlán, Mexico
1973

Walking along the beach with my girlfriend, Luci, one rainy Sunday afternoon, three boys glided across the ocean in front of us, standing on something that looked like a long, flat ironing board. They didn't look much older than I was. One of them was a very tall, very pale gringo. The other two were Mexican boys I didn't know. The ocean was alive with huge swells caused by the incoming storm. I was transfixed with the magic of people dancing on water.

Luci and I had been fighting about me holding her hand. She thought that if I was her boyfriend, I should want to hold her hand all the time. I told her that if she would let me kiss her, then I would hold her hand. As usual, it turned into a fight. I turned to her and said, "See those guys in the ocean? I'm going to do that. And if I like it, I'm going to do it forever."

Luci laughed at me and at the boys standing on top

of the water. I knew she didn't believe me. I wondered if she loved me, even though she said she did.

"If you don't love me, then leave me. I will join those guys and love the ocean instead."

• • •

It all started at the military school. I had so much work to do, and I began to think that flying was my escape. I had such a wish for flying, I couldn't shake it. I started to dream about flying as soon as I closed my eyes at night. Thinking of gliding through the air gave me a kick-in-the-ass feeling so that soon everything started to look like flying in the back of my head.

I walked Luci home and couldn't stop thinking about the people I saw riding the waves, about flying on top of the ocean, my feet planted on the board beneath me and my arms stretched out, holding me steady against the wind. Finally, I turned to her one more time and said, "If I am going to leave you for something, it will be for riding waves in the ocean." I was thirteen when I discovered surfing, girls, quaaludes, and weed.

I couldn't wait to tell my friend Nolas. Nolas lived with his mother and seven brothers and sisters in the house behind me. He and I were good friends at school and in the neighborhood. We were both good students, athletic, and daring to the point of being reckless. We were just finishing our second year at

Secondaria Miguel Hidalgo. Nolas was as fascinated as I was with this new sport. It was all we talked about.

Most people in Mexico have a nickname in addition to their formal name. I was called Chanfles. People still call me that when they see me on the street, in honor of my left kick, so strong that it made a soccer ball spin. That move was my trademark.

Nolas' name came as the result of the many times he tried to touch his girlfriend's *chichis*, only to have her cover her chest and yell, "*No las mamis!*" Nicknames in Mexico are all in fun, even when they sound terrible to people from other countries.

Nolas and I were especially eager for the school year to finish in June. Walking to school along the sidewalk in front of the beach, we couldn't take our eyes off the tourists with long surfboards, laughing and teasing each other along the seashore. We wanted to be like them. They were a new kind of athlete, standing straight and strong on top of the water as they rode their boards into the shore. They looked like a species of large, graceful birds riding the waves, flapping their arms for balance. Or, as was more often the case, diving into the water moments before losing their balance and plunging haphazardly into the sea. They were happy and carefree. Watching them made me happy, too. Thinking that I could be like them gave me a thrill.

I asked my brother Pablo if Nolas and I could use a surfboard he had stashed in our courtyard. Pablo never used the board. He just liked to accumulate objects to sell someday. Pablo let us borrow his board, and Nolas and I carried it along the sidewalk, from our house to Pinos Beach. The sea was choppy and foamy as I put the board in the water, climbed on, and started paddling out to where the waves were beginning to break. As soon as the first big wave reached me, I jumped up on the board and rode it all the way into shore.

It was love at first ride. Electricity lit up every fiber and muscle in my body. I was flying! From then on, I rode the waves all day, every day, whenever I wasn't in school. And even when my body was in school, my mind was in the ocean.

I was always a joyful boy. In the ocean, I became a peaceful, satisfied person. I knew I wanted to surf forever. I loved the power of the water as waves dashed against the rocky shore. With every wave, I wanted to get better and better. The ocean became my coach, my new girlfriend, and my best friend.

The school year ended in the middle of June, and soon three other surfers found us on Olas Altas Beach—Checo, Paco, and Lobo. We were the same age, and we named ourselves the Olas Altas Crew. We were the brown-skinned boys of that endless summer. Nothing about our previous lives fit us anymore. The ocean became our common home and the only schoolroom that mattered to us. The currents and tides were our alphabet, spelling out lessons that stayed with us for the rest of our lives. The clouds, the winds, the rain—these were our beloved textbooks.

As the Olas Altas Crew, we spent every available minute at the ocean, traveling from one beautiful sandy beach to another, in search of the biggest, fastest waves along the Mazatlán coastline. Our hearts sang with the pelicans, seagulls, and *tijeras* that swooped and laughed over our heads. We identified with the ocean creatures who shared our waves: dolphins, seals, jellyfish, and turtles. Neptune and Poseidon were our gods. Eddie Aikau, the legendary Hawaii surfer, was our hero. We declared ourselves protectors of each other, the ocean, and the earth. It was a perfect life and we knew it. We wanted it to last forever.

10
Checo

Tourists on the beach stopped to watch us surf. We became celebrities, as people asked to take our pictures and make Super 8 videos of our rides. While the rest of the Olas Altas Crew went to their classes, I started skipping school. Surfing was my passion. It quickly became my obsession.

Waiting for the next set of waves to reach us, we bobbed in the water and talked to other surfers, mostly tourists from the United States. We liked being part of the new surfing community. We knew enough English to talk and joke with them. We wanted to know about the United States and Canada, exotic countries far away from our daily lives. We loved setting up contests and tournaments of daring and skill, always trying to be the best surfers in the water.

Checo and I were especially good competitors. We enjoyed the challenge of conquering a new surfing trick. We laughed at the sense of danger that came from riding inside the barrel and coming out the other end. We celebrated as we learned to ride waves taller than we were.

I was a "right footer." I planted my left foot on the front of my eight-foot board and guided the board from the back with my right foot. Unlike most surfers, Checo was a "goofy footer." With his right foot on the front of the board, he expertly steered the board with his left foot.

Checo was short, dark, and well built, his hair burned brown by the sun. We all thought of him as the precious gem of our crew. He was the most handsome, in a Marlon Brando sort of way, and the best student. He was a natural leader, with total confidence in his athletic ability. When we were hungry, Checo would shimmy up a palm tree and grab coconuts and bananas for us to eat. He was undoubtably the best surfer, the one we all tried to beat.

The tourists admired our determination and our technique. They wanted to know about our lives, which I guess they thought of as exotic, even if they were normal to us. The tourists liked us for another reason. Because we knew every rock and cave near the ocean, they learned to depend on us to carefully conceal their drugs from the police.

Marijuana grew wild in the nearby hills, but stronger drugs started showing up in the early 1960s, brought by California men who had been in Vietnam and drug dealers from Tucson, eager to expand their territory.

It was only a matter of time before the tourists introduced us to the drugs they brought to Mexico from the US—uppers and downers, heroin, cocaine, and quaaludes. Although we were curious, we didn't start using heavy drugs for a few more years.

Marijuana was our drug of choice. It was easily available on the streets where we lived. We loved the feeling of relaxation we got from smoking weed. We smoked it all day long. We learned that with just a few hits we could talk to anyone. We were willing to lie to our parents, if necessary, to exploit our new-found sense of freedom.

Our drug use was never rowdy or reckless. For the most part, our parents overlooked what we were doing as long as we were quiet. We were careful and didn't allow our parents to see us drunk or stoned. Paco's mother, who was originally from the United States, told us, "If you boys are drinking, don't let me hear you." We were very respectful of each other's parents, especially the mothers, and we left the sisters alone.

My father and my friends' parents were proud of our increasingly proficient skills as surfers, but my mother hated what I was becoming. I was no longer a serious student, and my mother was furious. She continually threatened to throw my surfboard in the trash. I knew she meant it. Mamí and I fought all the time. I began not going home at night, mostly staying at Checo's house to avoid the constant fights.

My father missed me at home and often chided my mother, "Zelmira, leave the boy alone. He is becoming a man."

My father knew me well. Many times he predicted what was to come. "Neto is the one who will take care of you when you are old. The other boys are useless. Neto is a kind, loving boy. Please don't chase him away."

I finished *secondaria* and enrolled in Prepatoria General Rosales High School the following September. I was required to take only two classes a day as a student in *prepa*. I chose early morning classes so I could jump in the ocean and ride the waves by eleven. Every day, I brought my shorts to school, ran to the ocean, bummed a board, and jumped in the water.

I finished the first year of high school but dropped out early in my second year. The situation at home was miserable, and I couldn't see any reason to continue going to school. I was no longer a good student. I was only interested in being a competitive surfer.

When my mother made good on her promise to throw my surfboard in the trash, and the trash truck took it before I got home, I exploded. "How could you do such a thing?" I demanded. "My board is everything to me. I love it more than I have ever loved anything. More than I love you or the rest of my family," I yelled at my mother.

At the age of fourteen and a half, I left home and made my way to Tijuana. I crossed the border into the US, hiking across the desert from Tijuana to San Diego. I took a bus from San Diego to my cousin's home in Los Angeles, went to night school to study English, and was deported four months later when the police raided my high school. I returned to Mazatlán, eager to join Nolas, Checo, and the crew and go back to surfing full time. I never went back to school again.

11
Jáime and Marta

Inglewood, California
1974

I watched my cousin Jáime Rodriguez round up Tia Valvina's cows and herd them into their corral. He was quiet and content as he rode Polomo, his white horse, through the gate. The day was almost over. Valvina would be cooking something wonderful for their large family to eat. Maybe arroz con pollo or his favorite, carne asada with beans and rice on the side. Jáime was eager to get all the cows in the corral so he could close the gate and go home to a cold shower before dinner.

Jáime, the oldest son of my Uncle Gero and Aunt Valvina, was seven years older than me, about the same age as my brother, Pedro. But Pedro was a *flojo*, a lazy flounder, while Jáime has always been strong, brave, and charming. He was handsome and daring in the Rodriguez way. I often wished I could trade him for my oldest brother.

Suddenly Polomo started leaping and jumping like the devil with his pants on fire. Maybe the horse had been bitten by a bee. Or maybe the wind spooked him. Jáime was an excellent *vaquero*, but even he couldn't stay on Polomo this time. He was tossed over the horse's head and landed on the hard packed ground with a loud thump.

As soon as Jáime left the saddle, Polomo galloped out the gate and down the road, away from the corral, the house, and his rider. Jáime hit the dirt, sprang back up as if he was on a trampoline, and ran down the road after Polomo, yelling and calling him names. The horse kept on going and didn't come back until the next day. Jáime finally turned around, embarrassed to face all of us who had seen the circus. We were still laughing as Jaime limped up the road.

I looked up to my cousin when I was a kid. I knew I was going to miss him when he left La Hacienda as soon as he turned eighteen. Jáime told us that when he finished high school, he would go to California to work as a *bracero* in the orange groves of Modesto and the grape vineyards of Paso Robles. Being a picker was hard work, but he wanted to earn money to send back home to his parents, who still had a lot of younger kids to raise.

• • •

The summer I was fourteen and Jáime was twenty-one, he came back to La Hacienda for a visit. I couldn't wait to see him again. I wanted to hear his stories. I was eager to learn about life in California. *What were the people like? Did everyone speak English? Did everyone like to surf, like I did?*

I convinced my mother to take me and my sisters to La Hacienda so I could see Jáime again, before he went back to California. My cousin was happy to see me. Maybe he thought of me as a younger brother. I like to think that he did.

I soon realized that Jáime had come to see his family but also to see his girlfriend. Marta was already at La Hacienda that day when my family arrived on the bus from Mazatlán. We liked her right away. She was warm and comfortable and very much in love with Jáime. *It must be hard for them to live so far apart,* I thought as I saw them holding hands.

We called Marta "Wild Woman" because she was pure Indian, from the same small ranchero inside the *sierra*, where Tia Valvina was born. I'm not sure which Indian group she belonged to—maybe Huichol or Cora.

Like Valvina, Marta grew up picking plums from the many orchards that grew in the rich mountain soil. She had long, straight black hair, a face that was round like a full moon, an easy smile, and beautiful tan skin. Marta was a strong, husky young woman. She was wearing her native clothing when I first met her—a long, white, baggy dress. Her black hair was tucked behind her ears and combed straight down her back, almost to her waist.

Jáime and I talked every day, often late at night, about his life in California. He told me that I should come to Los Angeles. He made the trip sound like a great adventure.

"Neto, you are smart and brave. You speak English better than me." He smiled when he saw that I was listening carefully. "Come to the US and bring my girlfriend, Marta, with you. The trip is not that hard," he assured me.

Jáime had a work visa and could cross the border legally, but Marta and I needed to sneak into the country with all the others who didn't have legal papers. In the early 1970s, there were a lot of people migrating to the US, especially to California. Young men easily found work on the farms and in the vineyards and then sent for their families to join them and start a new life.

"When you get to Los Angeles, you can live with us for three or four months," Jáime promised. "I'll put you in night school in downtown Inglewood. If you like the waves in Mazatlán, you will love surfing in California."

"How can I bring Marta with me all the way from La Hacienda?"

"Call me whenever you are ready to make the trip. You don't have to go get her. I'll make sure that Marta is waiting for you in Tijuana."

• • •

That October day when my mother threw my surfboard in the trash, I knew it was time for me to go. I secretly called my cousin and told him I was coming.

"Jáime, I want to come to California. Do you still want me to bring Marta with me?"

"Certainly, Neto. Pack your clothes and come as soon as you can. Marta is already in Tijuana, waiting for someone to help her cross."

I spent less than a week getting ready. I told the Olas Altas Crew that I was leaving to go to the US. "Why are you going to do that?" they all wanted to know. They were happy to stay in Mazatlán, but I was ready for something new.

"I want to learn English. I'm going to bring back some new boards," I lied.

"How are you going to get there? Where are you going to stay? How are you going to get money to buy boards? When will you be back?" My friends had a thousand questions that I either couldn't answer or didn't want to.

When the day came for me to leave, I packed a little food and 300 pesos (about thirty dollars) in my backpack. I knew that soon it would be winter in California and that it would be a lot colder than Mexico. I added warm sweatpants, a sweatshirt, and a jacket. I told my father that I was going surfing, and I walked out the door. I was gone. I was free. I didn't say goodbye. It took a few days for my family to realize that I was not coming back.

I hitchhiked to Hermosillo, a big city about 885 kilometers north of Mazatlán. From there I made a deal with a bus driver to ride to Tijuana for a reduced fare. I found the Tijuana Hotel, where Marta was staying, just like Jáime had said. She had taken a bus from Rosario to Mazatlán and then to Tijuana.

Marta had about $150 in her purse, in case we needed to pay coyotes to take us across the border. I still had a few pesos in my pocket to help pay for our journey. She was sitting on a bench outside the hotel as I walked up the street.

I was happy to see Marta, but I was not prepared for what I saw. There she was, just as I remembered her, still dressed in her native clothes—the long white skirt, a long-sleeved blouse decorated with lots of colorful embroidery, sandals, and a cape over her shoulders.

I didn't know what to say. "Marta, I can't cross you into California dressed liked that. We'll get picked up right away."

"'What are we going to do?" I was afraid she was going to cry. "This is all I have."

"Do you have any money?"

"*Si*. I have all the money that Jáime sent me.

"You need to give me some of your money so I can go to the store to buy you a disguise."

"A disguise?"

"We will braid your hair, so you look like an American Indian. And people need to think we have known each other for a long time, so we have to talk to each other a lot. Pretend that I am your nephew."

Marta was nineteen years old, five years older than me, but she did what I said. I was the boss, and besides, I was taller than she was.

I made a quick trip to a store and came back with blue jeans and a shirt, black sweatpants, a yellow sweater, a warm jacket, and a duffle bag. Marta put on the clothes and looked uncomfortable.

"I'm sorry, Marta. You need to be a different kind of Indian. Try to get used to these clothes. You are going to be an American now."

My uncles Chendo, Gero, and Ramón worked as braceros in the orange groves of California in the 1950s and 60s. I thought of them as Marta and I got ready to make the trip. I told myself that we would be traveling along the same roads they had, as we made our way to Inglewood, California. I felt their spirits walking along beside us, telling me everything was going to be okay.

I met people in Tijuana who had already made the crossing several times and asked them what we should do. Back then, it was easy to cross into the US. The border was as porous as a sieve. Lots of people went back and forth between California and Mexico without official papers. Migration from Mexico to California was unstoppable.

Coyotes were available to guide people into the US who could pay their fee, but I just used my own wits.

Was I afraid? Maybe I was, but I didn't care. I knew I could make it. I was not shy about talking to people. I had been reckless and daring all my life. Going to LA was exciting. For years I heard stories about people crossing to the US, and now I was one of them. This was just another high for me.

Marta and I, and about thirty other people, slipped through a hole in the fence at three the next afternoon. We scattered as soon as we got on the other side. There were no guards at the fence, and the hole in the fence was enormous. Thirty people slipped through easily. Two horses could have walked through the hole without having to duck their heads.

With only a couple of guards on duty every day, the border patrol was no match for people running in every direction. Agents were mostly stationed at high observation places along the route, but the land was wild and hilly, with lots of places for people to hide. There was no modern technology like there is now. The agents only had their eyes and ears and a pair of binoculars.

At first, Marta and I ran like wild horses. Most people took the path on the right side of the highway, but we stayed left, along the side of the road that was less patrolled by the agents. At one point we saw two immigration men on horseback. We ducked down behind bushes along the side of the road, and they passed by us. Maybe they didn't see us. Probably they didn't care.

Marta and I walked quickly along a narrow, dusty path just below the San Isidro highway. There are irrigation tunnels at certain points under the highway, to stop the flow of fast-moving rainwater. Marta and I walked along the well-worn path and waited quietly outside irrigation tunnel number two, where we were told that a coyote would come with a big van to take us to the San Diego train station.

Marta and I talked as we walked along the path to the tunnel. Maybe we walked for an hour. Maybe less. The time passed quickly as we talked about growing up, our families, our hopes, and our dreams for the future. Mostly, I talked about surfing and she talked about Jáime.

We walked through tunnel number two, crossing from Mexico into the United States. Soon after we got there, a van arrived. We paid twenty dollars apiece and jumped into the van with seven other people. The van driver dropped us off at the San Diego train station at 5:00 p.m., and we boarded the train bound for Los Angeles.

This was the first time either one of us had been on a train. Marta was smiling and laughing as we walked down the aisle to our seats. I sat by the window and watched the sun begin to set on the water. There was the Pacific Ocean, the same Pacific Ocean that I grew up in, right in front of me.

The ocean was just as beautiful as back home. Huge, rolling waves crashed against the rocky shore.

The same seagulls and *tijeras* screamed overheard, diving into the water for food. The shore was filled with skinny birds on long legs, digging into the sand. I imagined sand crabs inching their way into rocks and crevasses, just like they did in Mazatlán.

The sun flooded the sky with rays of orange and pink before it made its final drop into the water. Later that night, I saw the moon rise in the sky, a full circle of light against a sky full of stars. I wanted to howl like a wolf, I was so happy and worry free. The world was mine. And then I remembered my father. I wondered if he was looking at the very same moon and maybe thinking of me, too.

At 6:15 p.m. we arrived at the San Clemente Amtrak station. We were almost home! We had one last hurdle: the San Clemente checkpoint. Migrants in Tijuana warned us that this was the place where most of them had been apprehended and deported back to Mexico.

The train stopped in San Clemente, and an immigration agent boarded the train. He gave a quick speech about telling the truth. He said that he would deport anyone on the train who was entering the United States illegally. As he stopped to talk to us, he looked me in the eye and shook his head. I knew Marta was shy and afraid. It was my job to do all the talking. Marta spoke two languages, but English wasn't one of them. When she was nervous, even her Spanish was hard to understand.

The officer looked menacing, but he spoke softly to us as he asked the standard questions. I was prepared.

"Are you two related?"

"Yes, sir. She is my aunt."

"Where are you going?"

"We're going to Inglewood," I replied. "I go to night school there."

That wasn't exactly the truth, but I intended to go to school when I got there, so it was almost true.

"What about her? Is she going to school, too?"

"No, she's going to meet her husband, my uncle, who works picking grapes in Paso Robles."

I was surprised at how easy it was for me to lie. With every question the agent asked, the lies got easier.

"Where are you from?"

"We are from La Hacienda del Tamarindo, near Rosario."

That, also, was sort of true. We both had family in La Hacienda, and I was sure the agent had never heard of it. I didn't want to tell the truth. Mazatlán was already getting a reputation for drugs, and I didn't even know the name of the little ranch where Marta was born.

That was all. The agent moved on. We were not detained. It was easy. Much easier than I had imagined. But this was 1974. Everything changed in the late 70s, when more border patrol agents were hired to seize drugs being smuggled into California from Mexico. We relaxed as the train pulled away from San Clemente on its journey to Los Angeles. Two hours later, the train pulled into our final destination.

I called Jáime from a pay phone and told him where we were. "*Primo, estamos aqui.* We are here, cousin."

"Where are you now?"

"Outside the train station in LA"

"How's Marta?"

"She's fine. but we're both hungry. What do you have for us to eat?"

My cousin laughed and told us he had fresh tortillas, chicken, rice, and beans. We would have plenty of tacos to eat as soon as we got to his house.

Jáime told us to look for a bus going to Inglewood. We got off the bus on Manchester Street, by the Forum. We walked about half a block, and there, standing in the doorway, was my cousin, arms wide open to welcome us home.

When I think back on this trip, I realize that one afternoon changed all three of our lives forever. For Jáime and Marta, it was part of their tender love story. They began a life together in a small village in Mexico and reunited in the United States, where they were happily married, raised four sons, and eventually became American citizens.

And for me, it was the beginning of my life on

the border between the United States and Mexico. I stayed with Jáime and Marta for four months, while I went to night school and learned English just like I said I would.

12
Teacher Becky

I was happy to go to school. I had come to the United States to learn English, and I wanted to get started. School began in September, but I didn't arrive until October. I knew I had to study hard so I could catch up.

My cousin Jáime enrolled me in night classes at Inglewood High, across the street from the Forum, where the LA Lakers practiced and played their home games. Night school went from 6:00 to 9:00 p.m. I had two classes, American history and English as a second language. Both classes were taught by Teacher Becky.

My teacher was from Santa Monica and pretty, in a California way. Tall and thin. I think she was about five foot ten, built more like a ballerina than like an athlete. She wore flat sandals, long skirts, and loose blouses to class every day.

I always wanted to know how old Teacher Becky

was, but I was afraid to ask her. She was a very strict teacher and didn't give out personal information like that. I found out from some other students that she had two daughters and that she been divorced for three years.

Of course I had a crush on my teacher, but I was shy and careful not to let her know that. Sitting in Teacher Becky's class made me want to be the best student in the class. I raised my hand a lot and usually had the right answers. I already knew some English from my surfer friend Paco whose parents were from the United States. Becky taught us polite phrases that we could say to people when we were not in school: "Thank you for your patience" and "Can you help me, please?"

Students from all over the world were in the adult education classes. I was one of many students from Mexico. Our classes were in both English and Spanish. I could easily understand my teacher and the other Mexican students. Listening to students from India and the Arabian countries speak English on top of their other accents was almost impossible. I liked being in school with Hindus, Muslims, and people from South America. I was becoming a citizen of the world.

All our books and papers were written in English. This served me well, later, during all the times I was in detention and read books to make the time go by faster.

I know I stood out from the other students. I was the youngest student and the most athletic looking. My hair was long and bushy. A lot of the other, older students wore turbans. I'm embarrassed to admit that I used to make fun of some of them, especially the Arabs. I called them "camel riders" because I didn't like the way they looked at me. They looked at me like I was different.

One day in December, Becky told me that she wanted to talk to me. I didn't think it was about my grades, but I was worried that I'd done something wrong. I worked very hard in her class. If I'd worked that hard in Mexico, I would have had nothing but tens on my report card.

"Ernesto," she began. "I hear that you are looking for ways to earn money."

"*Verdad*," I said. "That's right."

"Well, I'm looking for someone to babysit my daughters in the afternoon while I am teaching. My mother can watch them while I am at night school, but I need someone from the time they get out of school until five thirty."

"How old are your daughters?" I asked.

"They are nine and seven. They are good girls, and I know they would like having you as their babysitter."

I told Teacher Becky that I had experience taking care of my two younger sisters back home in Mexico. I would be happy to babysit her daughters. Honestly, I was amazed that Becky would ask me. She knew that I was a rascal on my skateboard. She knew that I spent time in the military school. I'm sure she knew that I was in the country without papers.

I was very protective of Becky's daughters, just as I had been with Alicia and Rosa. Every day I waited for them to come out of school and I walked them home, carrying my skateboard under my arm. They told me about school, and I asked them if they had homework. I made sure they stayed in the house and didn't go outside until their grandmother came to pick them up. If they were hungry, I made them peanut butter sandwiches and gave them something to drink. Usually, I made myself something to eat and drink, too.

If the girls wanted to watch television, we watched TV together. The girls liked to watch *American Bandstand*, but my favorite shows were the game shows where people won big prizes for knowing a lot of answers. The girls were tall and blond, like their mother. They asked me to tell them stories about my sisters in Mexico. I didn't mind if they giggled when I made an English mistake. Sometimes I made mistakes on purpose, just to make them laugh.

Life was good. I was living with my cousin and going to school at night. I liked my classes and loved my teacher. I was making money and learning a lot of English. I had plenty of opportunities to ride my skateboard around town and practice talking to people all day long.

When I wasn't in school, I listened to songs on the radio and taught myself the words. The Beach Boys were especially easy for me. I heard the melodies when I was surfing in Mexico, long before I understood the lyrics. Now, as I rode my skateboard up and down the streets of Inglewood, I sang the songs to myself and I knew those words. With my bushy, bushy hairdo, my baggy shorts, and huarache sandals, I was surfing the sidewalks of Californ-I-A.

But my favorite song, the one I sang at night after the house was quiet, when I came home from my classes, was a song I heard a lot on the radio that winter. It made me think of Teacher Becky, who truly was "just too good to be true."

And then, suddenly, my world turned upside down and backwards. It was February, my second semester at Inglewood High. Becky's mother was late coming to get the girls, and I missed school that night. The next night, when I was back in my usual seat in American history, everyone was talking about the race riot the night before.

Riots between the Black and Mexican gangs were common at Inglewood High. Some kids were being bussed across town to integrate the school, and they didn't like it. That didn't make sense to me. Coming from Mexico, where we rode buses all over town to go to school, I didn't see bussing as any big deal. Plus, If I didn't like someone, I stayed away from them. I was a good fighter, but I didn't want to hurt someone just because their skin was darker than mine.

I was in class less than ten minutes when police crashed in with German Shepherds on thick chains. Three strong policemen gripped huge, growling dogs that snarled and lunged in front of them. One policeman dragged me out of my seat, handcuffed me, and demanded that I walk ahead of him to the cafeteria, where other Mexican students were already standing against the wall. Teacher Becky and the rest of my class followed me out of the classroom and down the hall.

One of the Arabian students from my class pointed at me and said to the policeman, "I know Ernesto was part of the riot. I saw him fighting with a Black guy. Ernesto had a knife."

"Bullshit!" I yelled. "You are so stupid. Go back to the desert where you came from!"

Teacher Becky pulled the police aside. "Absolutely not! This cannot be true." She was shouting, which was not like her at all.

"Ernesto was not at school yesterday. I know he was not one of the boys who were fighting." She looked straight at me. "I know him. He is one of my best students. He was in Santa Monica, babysitting my daughters last night. He wasn't even here."

But the policeman wouldn't listen. He said that my name, Ernesto Flores, was on his list. The dogs were straining against their chains, thrashing and jumping at my face. I knew they would kill me if they could. I can't forget the nightmare noises of that night. Dogs barking. Police laughing. People screaming. Students begging as we were loaded onto two large buses.

I looked out at the street as my bus began to pull away. Becky reached up and spoke to me through the open window.

"I'm sorry, Neto. This isn't right." She had tears in her eyes and so did I. "I'll call your cousin and let him know where you are."

That night changed my life forever. I never saw Teacher Becky or her daughters again. The door to my dreams was slammed shut by dogs who would have ripped my face off if they had gotten loose. Instead, they tore my soul apart. For the first time in my life, I was scared. Fear tasted like vomit in my mouth. I hated the policemen who put me in handcuffs and arrested me. I hated the United States and all of its bullshit rules. I hated the Arabs, the gringos, and all the people who stood and watched as the buses left the parking lot. I was only fifteen, but I felt much older. I was never the same boy again.

The next day, back in Tijuana, drums beat furiously in my head and the angry words of Bob Marley rang in my ear. I no longer trusted silly California surfing songs or sweet love songs. Bob Marley and Peter Tosh were my new heroes. Their songs talked about revolution, and I listened.

13

Olas Altas Crew

Mazatlán, Mexico
1975–1978

The immigration van dropped me off in the middle of the night at the Tijuana Greyhound bus station, wearing only the clothes I wore to school that day. I was furious. A silent boy with no money in my pocket and no direction for my life.

The depot was empty, except for a few passengers waiting to board buses going back to the United States. I stomped inside, slammed my fist on the back of the wooden bench, and sat down.

Maldita sea! *What am I supposed to do now? I need money for food and a bus ticket back home.* Pinche migración!

I closed my eyes and let my nostrils flare like a bull, while I tried to slow my heartbeat and clear my head. I was too angry to sleep. I was hungry. I needed to piss.

At the first sign of sunlight, I pushed my way out the door, and stood, bewildered, in the nearly dark, slow-moving street.

My Tia Queta lives somewhere in Tijuana. How can I find her? How can I let her know I am here?

I watched as stores and street vendors unlocked their gates for the day. Men hurried along the streets and rode their bicycles to work. A parking lot owner opened the heavy, overhead door to his shop. A man in white boots hosed off the sidewalk before hustling customers to get their dirty cars washed for a hundred pesos.

"Do you need any help?" I asked the man in white boots. "I can bring in customers. I can shine cars for you. I can do anything you want."

"What are you doing here?"

"I just got thrown out the United States. I need to make some money."

"Okay. I can pay you for every car you bring in. And I can pay you for cleaning tires and shining wheels."

"*Gracias, señor.*"

"But, kid, you've got to smile. And take your hands out of your pockets."

For three days I slept in the park and worked in the car wash, earning enough money for food. I asked everyone I met if they knew my aunt and uncle.

One morning, as I finished buffing a man's shiny silver wheels, I looked into his eyes and asked, "Señor, I'm looking for my aunt, Queta Rodriguez. Do you think you might know where she lives?"

"Sure. I know Queta Rodriguez. She's a very kind woman. Her house is two kilometers from here. Do you need a ride?" I turned in my polishing rag, quit my job, and got in the man's car.

Tia Queta answered the door. "*Dios mio!* Ernesto Flores, is that you? What are you doing here?"

I told Tia my whole story. How I went to the US to learn English. How the police blamed me for being in a fight, even though I wasn't there. How the police handcuffed me, and dogs almost killed me before I was shoved into a van, taken to the detention center, and then dropped off at the Tijuana bus station.

"Do you need something to eat?" she asked.

"What I really need is a shower. And something to wear."

"Here's a towel. Go take a long shower. I'll have clean clothes ready for you when you get out."

Queta called her husband. Tio Jesús came home from the market with a new pair of jeans, a clean T-shirt, and a used backpack.

"Do your parents know where you are?"

"No, they probably think I'm still in LA."

"Call them from our phone and let them know you are here. We'll get you a ticket to Mazatlán. Tell your father you'll be home in a couple of days."

• • •

I missed my surfing friends while I was in California. I often called them from pay phones just to hear their voices. When I was deported and sent back to

Mazatlán, finding my surfing friends was the first thing I wanted to do. I was happy to see my family, but I was even happier to know that the Olas Altas Crew was still together.

The years from 1975 until 1978 were the happiest years of my life. The Olas Altas Crew was inseparable. We practically invented surfing in Mazatlán. We were the explorers, the pioneers. We surfed all the beaches and knew every rock hidden in the water. We were a community of reckless, grinning boys. We shared boards and encouraged each other. We didn't argue or fight or brag. We looked like a pack, but each of us had his own unique style. Most of the other surfers in the city were tourists from California. All of them knew our names.

"You guys even smell like each other," one tourist told me. "You all smell of salt and coconut oil."

That was true. We rubbed coconut oil all over ourselves, even in our hair, to absorb the salt on our skin. Our hair was bleached from the sun. Our bodies were tanned like leather. We were Mazatlán rascals, always smiling and having fun.

Riding the waves on my board, I became the jet pilot that I had always wanted to be. I sailed across the water like a bird. The waves were my air currents. I was a good pilot, totally focused on staying on course. There was just me and my board and the ocean in total concentration. No distractions or problems to deal with. Only endless miles, wave after wave, calling my name. I danced and sang. I couldn't help myself. As soon as I was back on shore, I walked out of the water, picked up my board, and went to find my friends.

After being thrown out of school at Inglewood High, I wasn't interested in going back to school with kids my own age and younger. My days of being in school were over. Paco, Nolas, and Checo were still high school students, but Donato, Lobo, and I were free.

We surveyed waves early in the morning, just as the fishermen were bringing in their catch. Los Pinos Beach, named for the pine trees that surround the shore, was the docking station for a fleet of fisherman who had been out in their boats all night. The morning silence was broken as they brought their catch ashore, ready to sell to markets and restaurants.

The fishermen's sharp knives flashed along the sides of the fish, scraping scales in one quick stroke. With a deep cut along the belly, they opened the fish, pulled out the guts, and threw them up in the air to screaming pelicans circling overhead. Meanwhile, neighborhood cats tiptoed across rocks where they had been hunting mice, and stood wide-eyed, waiting for someone to toss them an abandoned fish head or a boney tail.

We wished the fishermen *buenos días* as we walked between their boats, and they shouted back to us. We asked if they'd had good luck overnight. They held up their buckets of fish for us to see. They wished us good luck as we put our boards in the water and paddled out beyond the breaking waves. Our day was starting just as their night was coming to a close. Everything felt right. As soon as classes were finished for the day, Nolas, Checo, and Paco found us, and we were a family again, going from beach to beach, endlessly searching for waves.

• • •

I was fifteen when I came back to Mexico. Most of my friends had girlfriends. Nolas and Checo talked about kissing girls when parents weren't around. I wanted to have someone to kiss, too. I decided to find Luci Romero again. I was too lazy to look for someone else.

Luci was happy to see me, but every time I tried to kiss her, she backed away and yelled, "Neto, stop." If I persisted, she told me she would scream so loud her parents would hear her. So I gave up trying, even though both of us knew I wanted more.

One day, I was at Luci's house waiting on the sidewalk for her to come home from school. I heard Juana, Luci's mother, singing a song upstairs and knocked on the front door. I knew Luci wasn't home yet, but I wanted to see if there was anything I could have to eat.

Her mother answered through the window. "Neto, come in. I want to talk to you."

I climbed the stairs to the second floor and looked inside Señora Romero's room. My eyes popped open.

There was Juana, sitting completely naked in front of a short wooden table with a mirror attached. She was singing a slinky song and brushing her long curly hair. Juana was prettier than Luci, but with the same sweet, round face.

Of course, Juana could see me staring at her in the mirror. She swung around, the hairbrush still in her hand, and hissed like a snake. "Listen, *cabron*, I know what you want from my daughter. I don't trust you. Leave her alone. If you want something, you get it from me. Do you understand?"

I shook my head yes. I opened my mouth to say something, but nothing came out. My brain was frozen. I didn't even make a sound. I had never seen an actual naked woman before, and I didn't know what to say.

Juana stood up, pulled me over to the bed, yanked down my swim shorts and showed me what to do. I knew what sex was, but there were a lot of things I didn't know. We didn't talk. I don't think I even looked at her until it was over.

When we were done, Juana said, "Okay. Listen, *pendajo,* the next time you think you need to do this, come to me and leave Luci alone. If you touch her, I will tell my husband and he will kill you. I promise! Luci will tell me, and Carlos will stab you to death. Now put your shorts on and go home."

I still called Luci my girlfriend, but I never again tried to kiss her. I was afraid to even hold her hand. I went to find Juana three or four more times after that, but then I gave up. I loved surfing. Women could wait.

• • •

Surfing was not without its dangers, and we were a careless bunch. When one of us got hurt, we felt terrible. I stayed healthy, but in three years, Checo broke his arm and Paco broke his wrist. When an accident happened, all six of us, wearing surf shorts and carrying boards, trooped into the Red Cross hospital. We stayed together until our friend was bandaged or fitted for a cast, and then we left to go back to the ocean.

There were lots of times when we saved people from drowning. I can't tell you how many. I think there were at least fifty people over my lifetime. Lifeguards were in towers, but we were already in the water, so we were able to reach a drowning person first. Swimming frantically in groups of two, we sometimes saved two people in one trip.

"Look! Someone is yelling for help. *Vamanos!*"

With our boards underneath us, we paddled hard and fast until we found the swimmer, thrashing and sinking in the water.

"I'll dive down and get him. You stay here with the boards."

As soon as we got the drowning person to the

top of the water, we grabbed him around the chest, dragged him up out of the water and laid him flat out on the board, coughing and spitting up water. As we pushed the board to shore, people on the beach cheered for us. They called us heroes. I didn't feel like a hero, though. I was already in the water and I did what I knew how to do. The way I looked at it, I had already done enough bad things in my life. Saving people was a simple way to even up with God. It was a way to pay back for all the fish I stole, all the lies I told, and all the times I broke my mother's heart.

14

Donato

Birds write *Danger!* in large, swooping
letters across the sky. Suddenly silent.

The storm starts. An unexpected shudder
of cold wind and lightning flashes in a
far-away sky.

Thunder rumbles past, like an army truck
filled with soldiers holding automatic
rifles, bumping along cobblestone streets.

Drug agents in a tent high above the city
take cover.

Marijuana sellers scatter as the storm
approaches and the barrio goes dark.

Violence shakes the city. Everything freezes
in fear.

Palm trees bend to shake and sweep the
street. Dirt and sand whip the sidewalks.

Rain everywhere. In every direction. Strong,
sideways, howling sheets of water.

Tourists, in bathing suits and shorts, fresh
from the cruise ships, sit in hotel
restaurants, grimacing and hiding
behind their margarita glasses.

Waves crash against the seawall, flooding
stores and destroying thatch roofs.

Ugly, scrawny dogs cower and cry behind
boarded-up buildings. The fields offer no
shelter to anything not born here.

The birds are hiding, replaced by patio
furniture taking flight. Sometimes
crossing the street. Sometimes lost
forever.

The storm passes. Far out in the distance, a
lone, eighteen-year-old, red-faced surfer
rides fifteen-foot waves on his eight-foot
board.

Content and laughing. Happy to be alive.

• • •

Donato Swift, a boy from Redondo Beach, California, was the tall, pale gringo surfing the waves that day in the rain. I was just thirteen the first time I watched him glide across the water, as skilled as if he had been born there. I knew then that he loved the power of the ocean as much as I did.

Donato learned to swim in cold California waters and always dreamed of surfing the warm seas of Mexico. As soon as he finished high school, Donato drove to Mazatlán with his longboard in an old, battered Ford station wagon. We welcomed him into the Olas Altas Crew, and he quickly became our captain. Our mentor. Our guide.

When I told Donato what happened to me in Los Angeles, he told me what I needed to hear. "It will be okay. You will be okay. Hard times make good people," he said in his quiet voice. Even now, those words bring me comfort when I'm in trouble. They make me confident and strong.

Donato was built straight and skinny. I don't think he ever had enough to eat. His face was so red we called him Donato Tomato. He was generous and kind, energetic and funny. His American father met his Mexican mother, and they had two boys, bilingual in both English and Spanish.

I believe that everyone has a superpower if they look for it. Mine is that I never forget a face. Never. Ever. If I see an old friend on a street in a city far away, I recognize him right away.

"Hey, aren't you Cesár Valdez from Mazatlán? The kid who went to Escuela Juan Carrasco?'

"Si. That's me. Who are you?"

"I'm Ernesto Flores. We were in fifth grade together."

"*Verdad?* Is that right? No, I don't remember you."

That happens to me all the time.

Donato's superpower was that he was a clairvoyant, who knew what all the animals in the ocean were thinking. He understood the language of turtles, dolphins, sea lions, and lobsters. Sea urchins, starfish, jellyfish, and sardines. Every sea animal was his friend.

"If you commit your soul to the ocean, it will belong to the ocean forever" was his creed. It became my religion, too.

Donato made his home in an abandoned shack on Stone Island. It was our headquarters. Our campsite and our home. When I came back from the US, I often stayed with Donato overnight when my parents thought I was sleeping somewhere else.

During the day, if we weren't in the water, we all hung out at Donato's shack. We were fifteen and sixteen years old. We talked about girls, waves, and surfing. Our lives were simple: Get up in the morning, smoke weed, go looking for waves, surf all day, smoke more weed, find something to eat, talk about the waves we surfed that day, look forward to tomorrow, and do the same thing all over again.

Donato's shack was hidden in a jungle of palm trees, halfway up a section of Stone Island known as Goat Hill. The mango and banana trees kept us hidden from everything except the wild goats that roamed the hills, munching on grass and garbage. They watched us with their sleepy, suspicious eyes as we came and went every day.

Our hideout had four plywood walls and a tin roof so we wouldn't get wet in the rain. Donato stole a door from a work site and cut two windows in the walls for light and ventilation. We made a firepit and added benches made of stumps and driftwood from the beach. We stashed our collection of boards, mostly bought from tourists who didn't want to take them back home when their vacation was over.

I didn't smoke weed while I was in the US, but I started again as soon as I was back in Mexico. It was easy to get from the tourists in exchange for hiding their drugs from the police. We hid all sorts of illegal stuff for the tourists, but mostly marijuana and pills. Surfers from the US encouraged us to try anything we were curious about. By the time I turned sixteen, I had tried everything.

I especially loved the feeling of euphoria I got from Mandrax, a powerful Mexican Quaalude. Quaaludes were plentiful in Mexico in the early 1970s. They were legal with a prescription in the US and were often prescribed as sedatives, though probably not in the quantities possessed by the surfers on the beach. Quaaludes were eventually banned, both in the US and in Mexico, because they were so addictive. We quickly developed a tolerance that required us to use more and more in order to get high.

We smoked weed all day long. Being stoned was part of what made that time of my life full of joy. We asked around and learned that marijuana was grown in the quiet hills outside of El Quelite, about an hour away. Soon we were buying it for the tourists and taking some for ourselves. Donato found an old motorbike that we used to get back into the hills where plants were for sale. We made the trip often. We bought as much weed as we wanted, tied it to the back of the motorbike, and made our way back to Mazatlán in less than half a day.

One day it was my turn to make the trip. The path to the field was a half-circle, in and out of the bushes. It started at one point and returned a few miles farther up the dirt road. I was happy to be on the bike, making the trip to El Quelite that day.

I knew the ride back to Mazatlán would be peaceful and uneventful. I found the seller in the field, made the transaction, loaded the back of the bike with bags of dried plants, and started down the path. As I rounded the bend, six police officers stopped me, all of them pointing weapons directly at my head. They had seen me going into the semicircle and waited for me to come out the other side. Some of the police had clubs. One man had a pistol.

"Get off the bike, with your hands in the air," a policeman shouted at me.

I said nothing, as I slowly did exactly what I was told.

"This is the same *cabrón*, the one with the long bushy hair, that we see all the time on the beach," shouted one man to another. "I'm sure he does this all the time. Let's teach him a lesson right here."

I knew they were going to beat me, take my stash and my bike, and leave me bleeding in the road for someone to find.

I recognized one of the younger policemen. Roberto was from my neighborhood and had gone to school with my brother. I tilted my head up when I saw him, in a gesture that said, "*Qué pasa?* What's going on?"

"Leave him alone," ordered Roberto. "I know this guy. He's okay. He's young and stupid. Let's just take the marijuana and let him go."

I was lucky. Roberto saved me from being beaten that day and many times over the years. Whenever I tried to thank him, he just said, "Neto, get out of here before I take you to jail myself."

• • •

Marijuana made us hungry and Mandrax made us invincible. When the weather was bad or the waves were too flat to surf, we stayed out of the water and looked for something to do. Often we searched the ocean for fish. Taking turns with Paco's goggles, we took oysters from the bottom of the sea. The water was so polluted we couldn't see, but we could feel our way to the oyster beds. We would pull out a knife, scrape a bunch of oysters into our pail, and haul our dinner out of the water.

We set lobster traps in the water off Stone Island. Sometimes we would swim to El Faro, the lighthouse across the bay, and steal fish from the fishermen. We'd wait until their backs were turned, then we'd reach into their buckets, grab a couple of fresh fish, race down the dock, and disappear into the bushes.

The fisherman couldn't leave their boats to chase us or they would lose their entire day's catch to the pelicans. Now, I wonder if we were really getting away with something, or if maybe the fishermen didn't care. They knew we were hungry. Some of them had boys just like us at home.

The end of the day was a special time. We were hungry and thirsty, and we ate well. We cooked our food in front of Donato's shack on an old rusty grill, hauled up from the beach. We ran home for coolers of ice, fresh tortillas, and lemonade made by some-body's mother. We picked mangoes and papayas off the trees in the jungle. We used an ice pick to poke holes in coconuts and passed each coconut from per-son to person.

The sweet, sticky flavor of fresh coconut wa-ter along with the taste of soft, fresh corn tortillas was a satisfying sacrament. It was our communion.

Donato's shack was our church. Our refuge. It was our sanctuary from the complicated world outside.

We sat together around our campsite for a long time after dinner, telling stories and breathing in each other's company, sometimes drinking beer or tequila stolen from home. With palm trees whispering gently overhead, beating angel wings, we told our secrets.

Checo talked about how his brother won the Golden Gloves championship in Guadalajara and was killed in an accident on the drive home. I told them about the years I spent in the military school and how Emilio died in front of my eyes when I was four. Lobo talked of wanting to know where his father was. Nolas worried about his sisters and wished his mother didn't have to work so hard.

These tender moments, watching the phases of the moon and an ocean of stars travel silently across the sky, was the only time that Donato talked much about his family or his life in California. We didn't ask many questions. I wish we had asked more. Donato was a smart guy, a philosopher. When he started to talk, we paid attention. We wanted to know more about our friend, who knew that oysters and lobsters could hear ocean currents and that dolphins and whales talked to each other.

Donato talked about other places he wanted to go surfing: Alcapulco, Bucerias, Puerto Escondido, Pascuales—a lot of places I had never heard of, and I had lived in Mexico all my life. Donato liked to travel.

He talked about how big the world was, and all the things he wanted to do before he died.

When Donato started to say things like "The people you love, and who love you, will not always be there," I knew he was talking about his parents, who died when he was very young. One night, Donato said, "Sometimes I think my heart isn't big enough for all the people I love. I know how to love but I don't know how to take care of the people I care about. I disappear and they think I don't love them anymore, but I do. I always will."

When he said that, I wondered if he was talking about his parents. Or his brother, little Jimmy, back in Rodondo Beach, being raised by an aunt and uncle. Maybe Donato was telling us that someday he was going to get in his old brown station wagon and leave us all behind. I knew that was true. Nothing good lasts forever. But it made me lonesome to think about, on those sweet summer nights as we sat outside, listening to the music of the surf, bouncing off rocks and sliding into the sand below.

PART 2

. . .

Sinners and Saints

15
Camila and Estrella

Mazatlán, Mexico
1977

I lost my innocence on Olas Altas Beach. I was seventeen when I met two gorgeous, barefoot girls from Santa Monica, lounging on a rough yellow blanket.

The girls sat by the seawall, next to the rocks. They waved to me when I came out of the water with my surfboard under my arm. Their *sirena* hair was wet— long, blond, and curly. Wearing bright, two-piece Hawaiian bathing suits, their eyes were as blue as the sky. They looked nothing like the dark-skinned girls I grew up with. They were mermaids to me.

The girls stretched their long, tanned legs and smiled as I walked up to their blanket.

"Hi, I haven't seen you here before? Can I sit down on your blanket?" I asked in perfect English.

"Hi, handsome. Of course you can sit with us. *Comó estás?*"

"*Muy bien, ahorita.* I'm good, now that I've met you."

I put my board down in the sand next to their blanket. One of them handed me a beer from her small red cooler. My skin was wet and salty from surfing. I took a long drink and sat back on my elbows. They handed me a towel to wipe the sand off my legs and I grinned. I liked these two American girls. They were lovely. They made me laugh.

"Who are you?"

Camila answered first. "I'm Camila. This is Estrella. We're from Santa Monica. Have you ever heard of it?"

"*Si.* I've heard of it. It's close to LA. I lived in L.A. when I was fourteen."

"Is that where you learned English?"

"Pretty much. But I've been learning it for a long time here on the beach."

"We're glad to meet you. Who are you?"

"My name is Neto. Thanks for the beer."

"You're welcome. Do you have any weed?"

I tried to be calm. I didn't want them to know that their behavior was shocking to me. A Mexican girl would never ask for marijuana. Or drink beer on a public beach in the middle of the day. *Who are these girls? And what are they doing here?*

"*Por supuesto!* Of course. I have some good stuff in a hiding place right near here. I can show you if you want."

"Is it really good?"

"It's from Mexico. It's the best."

I finished my beer. The girls folded up their blanket

and grabbed the cooler. I picked up their big green beach bag and put it over my bare shoulder They each took one of my hands as we climbed the stone steps up from the beach. Their skin was soft to touch. I was excited in a way I had never been before.

As we reached the top of the stairs, I startled myself. My hands were slippery with sweat.

The young, charming Neto was still in the ocean, laughing and riding waves. This new Neto, bashful and shy, holding hands with two beautiful, blond girls from Santa Monica, didn't know what to say. My tongue tripped over the teeth in my mouth. The Mexican flag rose in my shorts as I brushed against their skin.

"Are you sure you have some weed?"

"I wouldn't lie to you. It's right over there, next to the school."

We walked to the elementary school where I had stashed a half kilo of weed between two heavy rocks. We were careful not to cause the attention of people walking past. I pushed away the rocks, picked up my bag of weed, and handed it to Estrella, who slipped it into the beach bag.

"Come home with us and we can smoke this together."

"Where do you live?'

"Across the street, at the Muñeca Apartments, behind the Belmar Hotel."

This is a good day, I thought as I ran back to the

beach and picked up my board. I met the girls in front of the hotel, walked with them to their apartment, put my board in their room and stayed for the whole summer—surfing, having sex, and smoking pot with them night and day.

The girls were older than me. Camila was twenty-seven. She was taller, more serious, and built like an athlete. Estrella, twenty-six, was shorter and a little more round. She giggled lot, probably from smoking so much weed.

"You seem to have a lot of money. Are you rich?"

"Not really. We worked together in California and saved up our money for this trip."

Meanwhile, I earned money recruiting customers to eat at the restaurants on the beach, especially El Patio and El Marinaro. The restaurants paid me for every customer I brought in. Sometimes they paid in cash. Sometimes they paid in food that the three of us shared.

I taught the girls to surf, and we went to the ocean every day, looking for the best waves. The girls followed me from beach to beach, starting out in Olas Altas early, as soon as the sun rose in the sky. By nine, we were at Pinos, then at Stone Island before lunch. Afternoons, we went back to the Muñeca apartments to escape the hot afternoon sun.

My friends teased me about where I was and what I was doing. I didn't care. I was happier than I had ever been. I met the girls in June and didn't go back home until the end of August, when they left to go to Peru. Because there were two of them. I didn't think of Camila and Estrella as my girlfriends. We were just three friends who met on the beach.

16

Captain Guadalupe Pimienta

Pacific Ocean
1977–1981

My dad found me first, surfing at Pinos Beach, when he rode past on his bicycle.

"Neto! There you are. I wondered what happened to you." Papí stopped his bicycle along the boardwalk, as I looked up from the sand.

It had been great summer, swimming and surfing every day. I was a warm-water fish. No cares or worries. Only good times with friends—who, like me, had no reason to grow up.

"I found some friends. I've been surfing all summer."

"I'm glad you are safe. But *m'hijo*, you are going to be eighteen soon. It's time for you to get a job."

I was happy to see Papí. All summer I wanted to tell him where I was, but I was afraid he'd ask me to come home.

"They are hiring at the shrimp cooperative. I think you need to go apply."

I got a job at the shrimp factory right away, helping the chemist throw acid on the frozen shrimp, preparing them for packing into boxes to be shipped around the world. I didn't like the work. My hands were burned by acid and I wanted to be in the water. The factory pay was good, but I knew I wanted to be an ocean man.

The Mazatlán shrimp fleet is the largest in North America. Every year in mid-September, I watched the wooden boats leave in a long parade from the port out into the Pacific, heading north to Topolobampo. I dreamed of joining a crew and spending my life in the ocean.

Captain José Guadalupe Pimienta lived seven doors down from my family in our neighborhood, Sierra del Mar. The year I was seventeen, Captain Pimienta sailed with the rest of the fleet out of the harbor in his boat, *La Gloria,* but soon he turned around and came right back. Something was wrong. With the Harbor Master as his escort, he sailed to the Cooperativa de Camaron, the shrimp boat cooperative shipyard.

I jumped on my bicycle and rode to the harbor master's office, concentrating on what I wanted to say. This was an opportunity for me. I imagined how my life might be different if I could join a shrimp boat crew. I leaned my bike next to a coconut tree, ran my fingers through my hair, and stepped up to shake the captain's hand.

"Captain Pimienta, I am Ernesto Flores. I think you know my father."

"Are you Jesús Flores' son? From Papagayo Street?

"*Sí, señor.* Why did you come back early?"

"Something is wrong with my engine."

"Do you need any help? I'm good with engines."

"I bet you are. Your father is a damn good mechanic. The best in Mazatlán."

I smiled as Captain said that. I was proud of my father, and I knew what he said was true.

"One of my men just walked off. I need to get this engine fixed. Then I need someone quick and strong to operate the winch that lifts the *chango* out of the water."

"Let's go to your boat. I will help you fix your engine. When the boat is ready, I would like to go with you out into the ocean. I can be your *chango* man."

"I'm letting you know, Neto, that being on a shrimp boat is hard, brutal work. There is no easy way to do the job. You risk your life every day. You go long periods of time with no sleep."

"I don't mind hard work, *señor*. I've been helping my father in his shop since I was thirteen."

I quit my job at the shrimp cooperative the next day. We fixed Captain's boat and headed out to sea: the captain, the engineer, two mariners, the cook, and me. The other shrimp boats were already far out in the water. We headed to the Baja, past Los Cabos, and into the Pacific Ocean to capture gigantic shrimp.

I couldn't contain myself. My face was always in a silly grin. Sometimes I would sing out loud for no reason. My hair and face were toasted by the sun, my body soaked in sweat and salt water, every fiber in my body awake and happy to be there.

Captain was about fifty-five years old, younger than I am now. He'd already been a captain for thirty years. Although he was tall and his back was straight, he looked like an old man to me. His hair was a thick, white mop. Originally very light skinned, the years and the sun tanned his skin a dark brown and made his neck as wrinkled as an iguana.

I spent a lot of time talking to the crew, especially the Captain and the cook, Mulacho. I learned that Captain had two sons, already grown. He didn't want them to work on the boats. He sent them to school instead. One night I asked him about his wife, who died when his sons were very young.

"Captain, why didn't you ever get another wife?"

"I knew I would never find another woman to love as much as I loved Rosita. I decided to love the water instead."

"But aren't you sad without having a woman to live with?"

"Yes, Neto, I am always sad unless I am on the water. The sound of the waves, the moon and stars in the sky—these are the things that bring me peace."

Every sailor has a "mark" in the ocean. It is the way we always knew where we are. Captain was a master of marks. We usually sailed about forty kilometers (twenty-five miles) offshore. Captain would see a star and know exactly how far we were from the next hill—the next mark. He already knew our destination for the day. He had been a captain for so long that some trips were based on pure intuition. He knew about stars and seasons. We stayed out in the water for thirty days at a time, fishing the states of Baja California, Colima, and Sinaloa.

Mulacho was an excellent cook. He cooked for Pimienta before I joined the crew and kept cooking long after I left to surf the waters of Mexico. I don't remember Mulacho's real name. We all called him Mulacho because he didn't have any real teeth, only a set of false teeth that he took out of his mouth and put in his pocket. I liked helping Mulacho load the boat with supplies, including a hundred kilos of tortillas, before setting out for a month or more on the water.

The best smell of the day was Mulacho's cooking. He served food straight from the ocean to our mouths. He cooked fresh fish, turtle soup, marlin, scallops, abalone, and octopus. Together, Mulacho and I opened the scallops and searched for pearls. He showed me how to make alcohol by fermenting pineapples.

The worst smell of the day was each other. We were hot and sweaty. We hardly ever changed our clothes. We certainly didn't use deodorant. We went to the bathroom right off the end of the boat, in front of the seals who followed us from place to place, all day long.

One day my own smell was making me sick. Halfway across the Sea of Cortez going to La Paz, I decided to take a swim. I was hot and salty, and the boat was anchored while we rested between catches. I didn't tell anyone what I was going to do. I didn't ask Captain's permission because I knew he wouldn't give it to me.

I dove over the side of the boat with a big splash. I was so happy being back in the water, I thought it would be fun to play a joke on crew. They knew I was a good swimmer. They knew I could dive underwater and fix engines from underneath the boat. When they heard the splash, they ran to the side of the boat, waiting for me to surface. Instead of coming up right away, I took a gulp of air, stayed underwater for a long time, and then swam under the boat to the other side. Nobody knew where I was until I called for them.

"Hey, Captain. *Hola*. Here I am."

Captain was furious. "You better get your ass up here or a shark is going to get you."

I laughed. It felt good to be back swimming in the ocean. For a few minutes, I was Poseidon. I wasn't Neto. I was Neptuno.

Captain lowered a net ladder for me to climb. "Don't do it again or we'll leave you here."

Mulacho told me later that when they couldn't see me, everyone was scared. They didn't think I was funny. They thought I was dead. The Captain docked my pay and made me stay on the boat the next time the crew went ashore. He taught me lessons I will never forget.

Our boat, *La Gloria*, was a large, sturdy wooden boat with huge propellers. On a good day, with the wind behind us, we could travel thirty knots, or about thirty-five miles, per hour. That was as fast as the boat could go, traveling from one fishing spot to another. But when we were actually fishing, we trawled very slowly—only about five miles per hour, going in a circle every hour and a half.

The Captain was right when he told me that being a *chango* man was hard work. There is a large circular net on each side of a shrimp boat. In front of this net is a "door" that runs along the bottom and scares fish up and into the net. The big nets have metal bars across them to prevent sea turtles and sharks from being caught in the net as it comes to the surface of the water.

Then there is a smaller net, the *chango* net, that is used to sample what is being caught in each fishing spot. My job was to operate the winch, pull up the net, and quickly count the number of shrimp inside. Fifty shrimp in the *chango* net meant there would be about fifty kilos, or one hundred pounds of shrimp, in the large net.

I pulled the *chango* into the boat every thirty to forty-five minutes, around the clock. Those shrimp went into a basket for Mulacho to cook for our dinner. Overhead, I heard pelicans and seagulls screaming for me to throw them random pieces of fish that were caught in the nets.

When I counted a hundred shrimp in the *chango*, it was time to pull up the big net right away. Usually this happened about every four hours. Using the big winch, all of us pulled the net out of the water and locked it in place. The shrimp were trapped at the bottom of the net until we dumped the net in the middle of the boat. The crew quickly opened six vents, three on each side of the wooden boat, to allow the water to go out. That was the call for all of us to go into action.

Two hundred pounds of shrimp jumped and splashed all around us. They twisted and turned and squirmed. Some jumped high out of the water. We grabbed shrimp, often three of four at a time, snapped their heads off, sorted them and threw the headless shrimp in huge wooden buckets. We threw the heads overboard and shouted to gulls and *tijeras* as they screeched and dove for them.

The acid from the shrimp heads burned my fingers and ran down my arm. We sloshed the buckets of shrimp with ocean water and let the water drain out before dumping the shrimp into nylon bags. The saline water kept the shrimp from sticking together when we packed them in ice.

We sewed the bag shut with a large needle and

nylon thread before piling the bags, ten high, in *la bodega,* the holding tank. *La Gloria* had two holding tanks, with ice on one side of the boat and shrimp on the other. There was no refrigeration. In the winter, when the water and the temperature outside was cold, ice was enough to keep the shrimp frozen.

Once the net was empty and all the shrimp were beheaded and bagged, the rest of the crew went back to sleep until it was time to fish again. I didn't sleep more than thirty minutes at a time. I had to keep checking the *chango* around the clock. I saw the sunrise and sunset every day.

Only when I had guard duty did a seaman take my place on the *chango.* As a guard, I was on the lookout for danger. Shrimp boats breathe danger. I watched for nets to get hooked underneath. I listened for the chug of an engine in trouble and for the sudden gusts of a storm that could break a mast or even flip the boat.

As a guard, I could sleep for three or four hours at a time, a luxury for the *chango* man. I slept in a bunk bed, on the bottom bunk of three layers reaching to the ceiling. I had nightmares the first season. I would scream and kick the side of the bunk so hard I scratched my legs.

"What were you dreaming about?" the crew would ask. I had no answer for them. I was so tired, I slept without dreaming.

We were all alone out on the water and seldom saw

another boat. Captain had a CB radio so he could radio a tanker if he needed fuel or to talk to other boat captains. Sometimes, changing locations, I had the wheel of the boat for four hours or more. I kept my sharp eyes focused on the ocean, as my heart beat a happy song in time with the waves. In my head there was music without words. The music of endless water that only the boats and the birds could hear.

After about a month on the water, the *bodega* was full. Four tons of shrimp were covered in ice— and it was time to head to shore to sell some of our catch. Captain declared a short holiday. He called ahead to find restaurant owners who wanted a hundred pounds of shrimp or more. That way, he would lighten the *La Gloria*'s load and make sure we each had some money in our pockets.

We set anchor and the crew went ashore in a small craft loaded with frozen shrimp and high expectations. Usually I stayed to guard the shrimp boat while the rest of the crew went into town. I told the crew what I wanted, mostly cigarettes or some weed, and they brought it back for me.

While the rest of the crew was away, I untangled the nets and fixed holes that trapped small fish. I carefully watched for manta rays and released them when I could. Manta rays make a sound like a crying baby when they are caught, and their cries still ring in my ears today.

I loved the solitude on the water when the rest of

the crew was gone. Every salty breath I took made me happy. I used this quiet time to think, read, and remember. I read *Perfumo* and *Siddartha* and books about submarines. I was eager for Captain to get back so I could talk to him about the books I read and what I had been thinking about as I sat alone, listening to the waves splash against the side of *La Gloria*.

In the spring, as the weather warmed up, we sometimes had to buy ice before heading back to Mazatlán. The good season ended in March, when the weather became too warm to fish.

Being on the water and working with Captain, I earned a lot of money. The Captain paid me 6,000 pesos at the start of the trip and 6,000 when the trip was finished. I used my money to buy a surfboard and a new bicycle. I gave my mother 7,000 pesos to help her with expenses at home.

The first year I took three trips with Captain Pimienta and his crew. Between trips, we spent about a week on land before heading out again. In 1979 I went with Captain on four trips and then asked him to drop me off in San Blas so I could catch a bus back to Mazatlán. In 1981, my last year on *La Gloria*, I took my surfboard with me. I was on the water for five months, five trips in all. When the crew went south to Colima, I stayed in Puerto Vallarta to surf. As much as I liked working on the shrimp boat, I still loved surfing more.

Captain José Pimienta died in the mid-1990s as an old man. Time bless my eyes, God! I met Captain when I was seventeen. He was a master teacher. I embraced his knowledge throughout my entire life: When to fish and when to take shelter. When to run from waves at full throttle and when to slow down, study the stars in the sky, and greet the sunrise with a smile and a heart full of peace.

Adios, Capitan! Vaya con Diós.

17
Julian

I finished my first year on the shrimp boats with a lot of money in my pocket. Every Friday and Saturday night all summer, from sunset until early morning, I partied and danced on the sand. My life was exciting and full of joy. I knew every inch of that beach and most of the people who were there. Beautiful American women and rich Mexican girls came to mingle, smoke weed, and have sex.

Soft, mellow music from acoustic guitars accompanied the rhythm of the waves that bounced against the shadows. We talked and laughed in the moonlight, flirting with each other, telling stories and jokes, never fighting. Only enjoying each other's company.

It was there, on Olas Altas Beach, that I met a married couple, Julian and Nancy, from Portland, Oregon. Born in Mazatlán, Julian left the city years ago to go to the US. That summer, the summer of 1978, was the last time he came back to Mazatlán, even though he was married to a gringa and could cross the border anytime.

Julian was a body builder, short and muscular. He kept his dark hair cut short. His face was always shaved, his mustache always trimmed. He had narrow, green, cat-like eyes that squinted against the sun. He seldom smiled and he didn't like to dance. He'd rather sit by himself, away from the crowd, and keep a careful eye on what was happening.

"*Qué pasa*, Julian?"

"*Nada*, Neto. I'm okay."

But Julian wasn't okay. We all knew it. People whispered about him when they thought he wasn't listening.

"What's the matter with that guy?" People asked, but I didn't know what to say.

"Even when he is partying and smoking weed, Julian is too serious. If I had a pretty wife like his, I'd be happy all the time."

Nancy was full of joy. She skipped and danced across the sand in time to the music. Young and trim, with short blond hair and shiny blue eyes, every person she met was a new friend. Always relaxed and comfortable, Nancy loved Mexico.

"Neto, this is the most beautiful place on earth. I've never seen such beautiful people."

That was the way Nancy was. Every seashell on the

beach was a treasure. Every sunset took her breath away. Talking to her made me appreciate my country more.

"The sunsets send ribbons of orange and pink across the sky. I've never seen anything like it. I would like to stay here forever."

I knew that Julian was low on cash. Maybe that was why he never smiled? Why his forehead was never smooth? I had an idea that maybe I could help him.

"Hey, Julian, come here." The tide was rising. Girls started to scream and laugh as the water creeped inland, over their bare feet and up their ankles. I found a place for Julian and me to sit, on an outcropping of big rocks at the side of the beach.

"Did you ever think about bringing some weed back to Portland? I think it would be easy to do in your truck."

Julian looked down at the sand, at the foamy surf rising around us. He chose his words carefully. "Let's talk about it, Neto. How much are you talking about?"

"I think we could easily hide five kilos in my backpack. You and Nancy can cross legally. I'll hop out at the checkpoints. I know my way around. You can pick me up on the other side."

Julian took a deep breath before nodding his head.

"Damn, Neto. That's a lot of weed. If we split it and I sell my share, I could pay back this trip. I'd still have some drugs and money for myself to start over in Portland."

"*Cierto*. That's right. You won't have to worry about anything as soon as you get back home."

We agreed. We would bring five kilos of weed, a little more than ten pounds, back to the US in Julian's big, bright green Ford F-150. The street value of that much marijuana was about $5,000—a lot of money back then. We made a deal and shook hands. I would keep three kilos to use and to sell. Julian was going to keep two kilos for himself.

In the back of my mind, I was still pissed off at the American government for kicking me out of California when I was fourteen. By smuggling drugs into the country, I was going to get even.

I was crafty. I knew I could get away with it. Besides, I'd heard that the government was not serious about marijuana or cocaine coming into the country. People were coming to Mexico asking for heroin and flashing hundred-dollar bills. If I could smuggle weed, I could probably smuggle heroin and cocaine just as easily next time.

My friend Rabino heard about our plan and wanted to go along.

"Hey, Neto. I hear you are going to US with Julian and Nancy. Can I come along?"

"Sure, Radish. But why?"

"My life is a drag. I've always wanted to go away from Mazatlán. You've done a lot of things in your life already. It's time for me to do something different."

Everyone called him Radish. He was a little shorter

than me, with bushy red hair and a round, smiley, red face. He was my friend from Olas Altas, even though he was never a surfer. Like my dad, his father was a mechanic whose shop was around the corner from my house. Rabino was everybody's friend.

"You know we're smuggling marijuana, right?"

"That's what I heard. I can help you get it across."

"Okay, Radish. Glad to have you along."

I picked up five kilos of weed from my friends in the hills outside of town. Julian and I talked every day about crossing the border.

"With Radish's help, the trip will be easier. Now we have two backpacks instead of one."

"What else do we need to bring, Neto?"

"Maybe some fruit. A couple of *tortas*. Radish and I will have extra clothes. Two pairs of shorts, extra shirts, a sweatshirt, extra jeans, and sweatpants."

"What about me and Nancy?"

"You need to look like you are going to work. If you get stopped, you'll tell them you work in San Diego. You are just coming back from spending the night in Tijuana."

"What do I say we were doing in Tijuana?"

"Tell them you went dancing with your wife." I smiled at my own joke. "And let Nancy do the talking. Your English isn't so good."

Julian's fingers started to fidget. His eyes narrowed. He swallowed hard as he crossed his arms in front of his chest.

"Listen, Julian, this is going to be easy. People do it all the time. Just let me and Radish out of the truck before you get to the Tijuana gates. You drive through the checkpoint and meet us at the 7-Eleven parking lot in Imperial Beach at sunrise."

"And relax. The border police are going to remember this bright green truck. Try not to look suspicious."

At six in the morning on August 17, we piled into Julian's truck parked in front of Olas Altas Beach. Julian and Nancy sat in the front. Radish and I climbed into the backseat, with our backpacks full of weed between us. The truck's camper was mostly empty, except for sleeping bags and camping gear that Julian was taking home to Portland.

As we followed the coast from Mazatlán to Culiacan to Mochis and Navajoa, we joked about the summer we were leaving behind. We remembered the people we met, the parties, the food, the drinks, the drugs, the fun.

We crossed the border between Sinaloa and Sonora. Radish pointed out scenery along the way.

"Hey, there's a lot of cactus here. And not many palm trees. Man, this is a desert."

Julian and I looked at each other. We forgot that Radish had never been this far north before. Eagles circled over our heads, looking for roadkill. Lizards scurried into bushes along the way.

We stopped in Navajoa for food and gas, to pee and stretch our legs. Nancy and I took turns driving the truck when Julian needed a break. The roads were difficult. Trucks sped past each other, hitting their horns as they tried to get ahead. We dodged potholes and accidents along the way. Big trucks overturned on the hills when drivers fell asleep or brakes failed. We passed cars with flat tires and mechanical problems, but we didn't stop to help. We were on to Guaymas and Obregon.

"I'm glad to get out of this truck," we agreed as we stopped for dinner and a night in the motel. We'd been in the truck for twelve hours. The evening temperature dropped from hot, sticky Mazatlán to cool, dry Hermosillo. We had four more hours of driving ahead for the next day. Our big adventure was just getting started.

"Let's get going." Julian pounded on our door the next day before breakfast. We stopped for bread and coffee and got back on the highway to Mexicali, where we ate lunch and reviewed our plan for crossing into the United States.

Julian kept wanting to stop and pee by the side of the road. "Man, I don't know if it is the coffee or the nerves, but I need to take another piss."

I teased Julian and Radish. I didn't want them to know that I was nervous, too. I talked to a lot of people, but this was my first time to cross the river on my own. I was wary of thieves on the Mexican side and guards across the river. The water was deep and the current was strong, but the river at that point was narrow, only about twenty-five meters wide.

We pulled into Tijuana at four in the afternoon and found a restaurant, where we had dinner and a couple of beers. At eleven, Julian drove us to Playa Tijuana. We reviewed our plans one more time. Julian and Nancy would go back into town, drive across the legal immigration checkpoint, and meet us on the other side of the river at dawn.

Radish and I changed clothes in the truck, out of our jeans and into swim shorts and dark T-shirts. We tied up our shoes in plastic bags and put them inside the backpacks loaded with warm clothes and weed.

The Tijuana River was cold as we stepped into the dirty, waist-high water. Putting the backpacks on top of our heads, we steadied ourselves against the rushing river. Ten minutes later we were on the other side. We hurried to change out of our soggy clothes and into our tennis shoes, warm sweatpants, and sweatshirts. We threw our wet clothes into a pile of rocks, a graveyard for discarded wetback costumes, and walked along the trail to Imperial Beach in silence. Ever alert. Trying to stay calm.

Meanwhile, I pictured Julian and Nancy showing their legal papers at the checkpoint. I imagined Nancy in the driver's seat, smiling at the guard, answering his questions, and convincing him there was no reason to be suspicious.

Radish and I took turns resting on the beach and watching for intruders. Crossing the river was a rush. Both of us were too excited to sleep.

As the sun started to rise, we put out backpacks over our shoulders and walked a mile and a half to the 7-Eleven, but there was no sign of Julian or the green truck.

"Are you sure this is where we're supposed to meet them?"

"Yeah. I think so. This is the only 7-Eleven around here. Maybe they overslept. I don't think they would have left us here. We've got the stash. I'm sure they'll be here."

Suddenly, two flashlights came toward us. My stomach flipped over. *Please, God, don't let this be the border guards. Not now,* I prayed.

Radish started to shake. I put my hands on his shoulders and looked him in the eye.

"Don't worry, Radish. It's okay. I can take care of this," I said, and we ducked into the bushes.

Julian and Nancy came toward us, swinging their flashlights and laughing. "Here. We brought you some hot coffee. Our truck is around the corner. Let's get back on the road."

Our next stop, the big immigration checkpoint in San Clemente, was about an hour away. Julian eased his truck into the long line of cars waiting to pass the guard station. Me and Radish climbed out of the truck and jogged across the highway, the San Clemente cliffs directly below us.

I grabbed Radish by the arm. "*Maldita sea!* Goddammit! Immigration saw us. Something must have clicked in their heads to make us look suspicious. We've got to hide."

I could see surfers on the beach down below the cliff. They looked up, saw me and Radish running for our lives, and waved.

"Hurry," I yelled to Radish. "We need to climb the cliffs."

We scrambled sixty meters down the San Clemente cliffs with our backpacks over our shoulders, until we found a cave near the beach to hide in.

"Neto, I need to stop and catch my breath."

"Sure. No problem. We'll wait here for a while. But eventually we need to get back up there, to see if the police are still looking for us."

For the next thirty minutes we crawled like geckos, climbing up and down, down and up, from the beach to the top of the cliff, two or three times, taking a peek each time before going back to the cave.

But the police were always still there. Every time we looked, there they were. Still searching for us.

At last, back down on the beach, I saw a big biker walking toward us with his longboard under his arm.

"Hey, amigo. Where is the bathroom?" I shouted. The guy pointed.

We ran to the bathroom to change into surfer shorts and muscle shirts. We stuffed our jeans and T-shirts into a trash can and walked out into the sunshine. We spotted Julian's green truck in the parking lot next to the bathrooms, jumped in, and put our backpacks on the floor. This was the last checkpoint we had to cross. We were on our way to Portland.

We left San Clemente, driving as fast as we could without being noticed. We stopped in LA at a house of one of Julian's friends, but not to sell any weed. We just wanted a few hours of rest and something to eat. Three or four hours later, we were back on the road to Portland. Julian drove twelve hours straight. We didn't want to stop anymore. We'd had enough adventure. We arrived in Portland on a gray, rainy summer day, August 20, 1978.

We made it. I was on my way to becoming a bigtime drug dealer. I was going to make a lot of money, buy a lot of boards, and take them back home.

After the trip, Rabino disappeared. We never saw him again. I think he was killed somewhere in the hills near Portland. I wish I had told him not to come. He was a good guy who just wanted a little adventure. He didn't deserve to die.

18

Mario

Southern California reminded me of Mexico. Portland was a foreign country. There were no tall, swaying palm trees. Just a river and huge pine trees, standing straight and tall like soldiers. The days were cool, compared to the hot, humid days I'd left behind. The beach was ninety minutes away and too cold for surfing. The sky, the color of oatmeal, was not the bright blue sky that I knew. The summer sun didn't set until almost nine. There was a light that glowed on the trees before sunset, called twilight, that I had never seen before.

High in giant trees, ravens squawked back and forth to each other in *cuervo* language, short angry words bursting from their shiny black throats. *Maybe they are warning me of something?* I should have listened more carefully.

• • •

After Julian dropped me off, I needed a place to live and I needed a job. He introduced me to Mario, a guy from Mazátlan, who said I could stay with him and his wife for a couple of weeks. Mario was a creepy little guy with thick, smudgy glasses. Everything about him was ugly. His teeth were yellow and crooked. His hair was all scrambled on his head, and he had a silly mustache that made him look like a cartoon.

Mario's wife, Valerie, was born in Portland. She was a big person who talked loud and walked real slow. She was respectful to me, but I never found her very good to look at. Valerie's powerful presence at home made me uneasy. She frowned at everything she looked at, and it was hard for me to talk to her. I probably never spent more than thirty minutes with her the whole time I lived in their house.

Valerie worked as a dental assistant. When she wasn't wearing her white uniform, she dressed like a man, in baggy jeans and flannel shirts. She wore her hair in a ponytail, tied behind her neck, or in dirty strings across her shoulders. Out in the yard, she wore heavy man-boots and an army jacket to guard against the cold wind.

Living with Mario and Valerie wasn't easy. I had money in my pocket from selling weed, but I was bored. I hated being home with Mario during the day. He never went to work, and the house was filthy and rundown. Mario spent the whole day sitting on his ass, watching television and smoking weed. He was on welfare because he'd hurt his back in some kind of an accident. I think that's why he liked living in the US. The doctors gave him pain pills that didn't make his pain go away. They only made him paranoid and mean.

One day I told Mario, "It's a good thing you live here and the government pays you not to work. If you still lived in Mexico you'd be doing construction like the rest of us."

"But I couldn't work. It would hurt my back."

"*Por supesto*. Of course. Every man's back is sore at the end of the day. It doesn't matter. We still have to get up and go to work the next day."

Mario turned on the television as soon as Valerie left the house, and he kept it on until after the late news at night. During the day he watched quiz shows and cartoons—*The Price Is Right* and *Tom and Jerry*. At night he and Valerie watched comedies—*All in the Family* and *Happy Days*. He liked to think of himself as Archie Bunker, sitting in his big chair, mumbling and grumbling about the world. Talking about all the people he didn't like.

Mario's favorite show was *Charlie's Angels*. Right in front of his wife, he talked about Farrah Fawcett and her big tits. When he said things like "I'd like to give her an assignment," I had to leave the room.

One day, late in the afternoon, Valerie's brother, Todd, came to visit. He pulled me aside.

"Neto, I know you brought weed from Mazatlán. Nancy told me."

"That's right. Do you want some for yourself? Or to sell?"

"How much do you have?"

"All together, I have a little less than three kilos."

"I'm looking for some to sell. I know a lot of people around here. I can help you get rid of what you've got. How much do you want for it?"

"I can sell it to you for three thousand dollars, but you don't have to pay me all at once. You can buy it as you need it, and pay me back later."

Todd knew that he could sell what I had for $1500/kilo and make a good profit. A serious college student, not quite ten years older than me, he said he wanted to make enough money to pay for school. I'm not sure I believed him, but we made a deal and shook hands. I liked Todd and I wanted to trust him. He seemed like a good guy to me.

I was thinking about leaving the cold, wet place that was Portland, but Todd put his hands on both of my shoulders, looked me in my eyes, and told me to stay.

"Listen, Neto, I know you're not very happy here. But unless you have a good reason to go back to Mexico, I think you should give Portland a chance. We like you here. You are easygoing and the girls like you a lot. I can introduce you to some people who will help you get a job. What do you think?"

Todd started inviting me to go with him to the downtown bars in Portland. The legal drinking age was twenty-one and I was only eighteen, but I looked older. My hair was long and curly. I looked like everyone else in bell-bottom jeans and bright flannel shirts. I flashed a phony ID and the guard at the door let me in. After a couple of weeks, the bartender saw me so often he just waved.

Todd was right. He had a lot of friends. People paid attention to us when we walked through the door together. Todd with his blond hair and clear blue eyes and me with long black hair and dark skin. We were both good looking, muscular, and strong. I liked being with Todd, and I liked meeting his friends.

One night, Todd and I were standing at the bar, when two really tall guys walked in. They looked like lumberjacks I'd seen on TV. They shook Todd's hand and patted him on his shoulder.

Todd turned to me. "Neto, these are two of my friends, Mike and Mark, from Sandy."

I liked the brothers right away. They were agreeable guys, with big smiles and a confident energy. They asked me where I was from and what I was doing in Portland. I told them I was from Mexico. I didn't tell them that I was there selling weed.

"Who is Sandy? I never heard of her."

"It's a town." Mike laughed. "About twenty-five miles east of here."

"What do you do there?"

"I run a welding shop. Mark runs a gas station, and together we have a big strawberry field."

Both guys were easy to talk to. Their words were soft and warm. I felt like I could trust them, so I asked, "Do you know anyone who has work?"

"I can use someone to work with me in my iron shop. Do you know how to weld?" Mike answered.

"I've never done it, but I worked with my dad in his blacksmith shop when I was growing up. I'm a good mechanic. I'm sure I can do whatever you need."

Mike told me I should report for work the next day. My job was making large, iron racks for supermarkets. I liked using the electrical welder. It felt good to be working again.

When Mike offered me a place to stay, I said yes right away. I wanted to get away from Mario. The day I moved out, Mike asked me about living with Mario.

"He's okay, but I don't really like him."

"Well, if something seems suspicious, tell me right away, okay? I don't want anything to happen to you."

I moved from Mario's house into a big farmhouse that I shared with Mike, his wife, and their little boy. His wife, Maria, was a Blackfoot Indian woman. She was pregnant with their second son when I first arrived. She had the baby that fall, while I lived with them. Life was better as soon as I moved to their farm. Maria was smart. She was interesting to talk to, and I loved their little boy.

One day Mark came into the shop while I was welding. "Hey, Neto. I need someone to guard the strawberry fields at night. The damn deer are eating all my crops."

That's how I ended up working two jobs. I got up early in the morning to go to the welding shop. I rested a little after work, and then at night, I rode to the strawberry fields on horseback to scare away the deer.

I was never afraid inside the forest. On top of a beautiful white horse, I felt like a king guarding the strawberry fields. I loved the misty mornings that came with the sunrise. They reminded me of stories I read about castles and places far away.

Three or four nights a week I rode through the sloppy wet fields, carrying a pistol and a shotgun to scare the deer away. Once in a while, the fields were dry enough for me to ride a motorcycle, sometimes a quad and sometimes the two-wheeler, but always with the engine silenced. Every couple of hours I'd go out for fifteen minutes to do my round, checking for animals. Mark guarded on the nights I was off.

One night, while I was enjoying my solitude, sitting on top of my big white horse, watching for deer and not seeing any, I got the idea to help these brothers who had been so kind to me. I talked to Mark the next morning.

"Mark, I know a way for you to make twice as much money as you do now."

"Really? How?"

"You can grow marijuana in between the strawberry plants. The weather here is perfect. I can plant it for you and watch both crops at night while I am guarding the fields."

I was right. The climate was perfect. It rained just enough, and the temperature was never very hot. The strawberries had already been harvested. I planted this new crop in September and watched it grow tall.

I was busy keeping the animals away. Deer loved strawberries, but they loved marijuana more. I searched for their tracks and fired my shotgun in the air to scare them. I never killed any deer. I just wanted them to run away. They needed to stay away from my fields, not trample them.

My life was good. I was beginning to like being in Oregon. I was happy living with Mike and Maria, working in the welding shop during the day and guarding the fields at night.

In October, leaves began to turn bright colors I had never seen before—red, yellow, and orange—in between the giant evergreens. Sometimes, clouds hung low in the valley, waiting to send down rain across fields of slippery mud.

I celebrated Christmas with Mike and Maria, their two children, and Mark. It was one of the nicest Christmases I could remember. I was with a family again. There were presents under a real Christmas tree, cut down from the forest. Maria cooked a pot of spaghetti, and we exchanged gifts. We didn't go to Mass, but the night felt peaceful and holy. I went to sleep, content and optimistic about what the New Year would bring.

I had no idea how quickly it would end. People turned on me in the shadows. I was not prepared for so much danger and disappointment.

• • •

One Saturday morning in mid-January, I went to Portland to pick up warm coats to take back to the ranch. The temperature was cold at night, and we needed coats to keep us warm. I called Julian to let him know I was there.

"Neto, Mario wants to see you. Is it okay if I let him know you're in town?"

"Sure, Julian. I'll meet you in Sears parking lot about one o'clock."

I waved when I saw them drive up. Soon, we were laughing together. We were three guys originally from Mazatlán, talking about the past and people we knew. Julian and Mario were acting like everything was okay when, all of a sudden, I saw a reflection in Mario's sunglasses. A stranger was behind me with a knife, ready to stab me in my back.

"*Qué Mierda! Qué chingado está haciendo aquí.* What the hell is he doing here?" In a flash of the knife, I knew that Mario had paid this man to kill me. Julian had set me up. They were two miserable, hateful people whose only loyalty was to weed. They didn't care about me, their wives, or anyone else.

I spun around, twisted the man's wrist with both my hands, and took the knife away from him. I was jumpy. I had the knife in my hand. I knew I could kill him. I wanted to kill him. I wanted to kill Mario and Julian, too. I wanted to kill all of them.

My father's quiet voice sounded in my head. "Son, walk away. Don't get their blood on your hands. You will never be able to wash it off."

I acted normal and calm. "Hey, what are you doing? I don't want to start any trouble with you."

Mario looked at me with rage. "I know you are having something to do with my wife. You two are sneaking away at night and having sex behind my back."

"You stupid, paranoid, drug-addict fool. I'm not doing anything with anyone. I'm working two jobs. I hardly have time to eat, sleep, and go to work. I haven't talked to your wife in almost four months."

Julian got in between me and Mario. He grabbed my shoulders and pushed me away. "Neto, it's time for you to leave. This isn't the place for you. I'm going to take you to the bus station right now, and you are never coming back."

I was on the next bus to Mexico. I didn't say goodbye to Mike and Maria or Mark. I just left. I wish I had said goodbye to Mike's little boy. I hope Julian told them where I went.

I left Portland, with my soul so full of holes. I was leaking water. I had been in fights all my life, but this was the first time I had serious enemies. Mario hated me so much he was going to kill me. I was forced to leave a town I liked, a good job, and people I cared about.

Portland was a hard place to live, but I was happy. I had seen this different part of the world. Now I didn't know what to do with my life. I rode the bus back to Mazatlán, so angry I couldn't speak. I glanced out the window and watched scenery change from pine trees to palm trees as the bus raced down the curves of Highway 1, along the California coast.

When the bus pulled into Los Angeles, I put my jacket over my head and fell asleep. I wanted to be left alone. I was betrayed. I didn't know what to say.

• • •

Back in Mazatlán, I walked into my house and said hello to my dad, who was fixing dinner for Franco and Cachi. I could smell *ceviche,* the shrimp cooking in lime juice.

"*Gracias a Dios!* Neto, thank God you are home! I was afraid you had been killed."

"I almost was."

Papí hugged me hard. I rubbed away tears and hugged him back. He gave me a bottle of beer, and together we sat down at the table.

"Every night, I prayed to the Virgin Maria that I would see you again."

"I knew you were praying for me, Papí. I felt your prayers all the way to Portland."

I sat back in my chair, lit a cigarette, and looked up at a sky with no clouds. I saw yellow birds darting from tree to tree, squawking like parrots. An iguana climbed the walls of our patio, stretching her neck in worship to the sun. High above, an airplane left a white trail across the sky.

Shrimp boats were going to go out in the ocean. I found my friend, Captain Pimienta, and signed on. I was happy to be away from danger and to go back on the water. To be home.

19
Tijuana

My father was driving drunk when he crashed his car and sent it over a bridge outside Mazatlán. The transit police called my oldest brother to come and pick up the car, but no one knew what happened to Papí. His body was nowhere near the accident site.

Maybe someone picked him up the night of the accident? I whispered to myself. I searched Mazatlán for months, but no one knew where he was. I prayed every night for someone to help me find him. I knew I would never give up until I knew what had happened.

Two months went by. I was eating breakfast when Hermán Vega, my father's compadre, called to tell me that Papí was seen getting on a bus to Tijuana. If it was true, it was a miracle that Papí was still alive. But how was I going to get to Tijuana?

My brothers wanted to go to Los Angeles. To take

a road trip to see our mother and our sister Alicia. At the last minute they decided I could come along.

"Neto, jump in. You can help drive."

Like circus clowns, we jammed ourselves into Pablo's two-door AMC Pacer. I was the only one without a passport. The only one who wasn't legal. I couldn't cross the border in their car, but I could ride with them as far as Tijuana.

The weather was starting to warm up just in time for Easter. Pablo and I had been to California before, but this was the first time for Franco and Cachi, who were finishing high school.

We laughed and teased each other as we took turns driving straight through, from Mazatlán to the California border. We told stories. Cachi and Franco wanted to hear where I had been while I was away. I told them about working with Captain Pimienta on the shrimp boats. I told them about the summer I came in sixth place overall in the Mexican National Surfing Competition in Guerrero. I told them about the ten months I spent fishing for tuna and marlin, working and surfing in Pentacalco while I practiced for the next big competition.

"So, how did you do in that contest?"

"It was canceled because the waves weren't big enough." I stopped talking. *What would my life be now if I could have competed one more time?* I wondered. I dreamed of being the Mexican national champion. *Could I really have won the competition?*

A lot of people said I could. I shuffled my body in the cramped backseat. There was no use thinking about that now.

We traded places driving. I drove the stretch from Hermosillo to Mexicali and was laughing and joking when I saw a wheel come off an eighteen-wheeler tractor right in front of me. The wheel went rolling down the highway right toward us. A lot of people stopped to watch, but I reacted fast and just kept driving. The wheel was coming straight at me. I stepped on the gas and moved to the other side of the road. My brothers gasped a full breath of air as they slid in their seats.

"*¡Dios mío!* That was close. I thought we were going to be killed."

"It's okay. I'll take care of you." I laughed. But I was happy to let Pablo drive the rest of the way.

At eleven in the morning, twenty hours after leaving Mazatlán, Pablo eased his car to a stop at the US checkpoint, into the line of cars crossing the border.

"Sorry, *cabrones,* this is where I need to get out."

I climbed out of the backseat. It felt good to stretch my back and my legs before shaking hands with Pablo, the only one who wasn't asleep.

"Can you give me a few pesos? I'm going to look for Papí. Don't look for me in LA. I might stay here for a while."

I swung my backpack over my shoulders. I was a traveler again. The last time I had been in Tijuana was five years ago, on my way back from Oregon. That time I was angry and defeated. This time I had a mission. I needed to find my father.

"Good luck. Call us if you find him," Pablo called out the window, as the car crawled forward in the inspection line.

My father was sixty-five years old. If he wasn't here in Tijuana, I knew he could be dead. My stomach hurt. *I have to find him. He has to be here.* I shifted my backpack on my shoulders and forced myself to walk faster. I wanted to whistle, to believe that my father was safe, but my throat was too dry. I shook my head and took another step.

I needed to get to the Cañon Johnson neighborhood, about an hour away from my drop-off point. My cousin Iván Vargas lived there with his son Juan. Together they owned an auto repair shop. Cañon Johnson Boulevard was going to be my first stop.

There were a lot of people walking with me along Avenida Revolucíon, a busy, tourist street with lots of cantinas and souvenir shops. I stopped five different people on the street, asking for directions to Cañon Johnson.

"You're going the right way. Stay on this street and you'll get there."

At last, I was at the intersection where Avenida Revolucíon crossed Cañon Johnson Boulevard. I stopped a man coming toward me. He had a friendly face and was about my father's age.

"I'm looking for my father, Jesús Flores. Do you know him? Have you seen him?

"Are you looking for El Padre?

"No, El Padre is Iván Vargas. My father is El Tio del Padre, the uncle of El Padre."

"Sure. I know El Tio."

"Where can I find him?"

"Go to Bolas Mofles, the muffler shop. Next to that is El Padre's repair shop, where Iván fixes all kind of cars with bad suspensions. Fifty meters down the hill is Los Compadres liquor store. Ask them where your father is."

Gracias a Dios! My heart swelled with joy. I wanted to sing. To run and jump in the air. My prayers had been answered. This man knew my father. My father was alive!

I walked into Los Compadres, a twenty-four-hour liquor store. Outside, sitting on a wall overlooking the city were three men who introduced themselves as El Caballo, El Burro, and El Camelo—the horse, the donkey, and the camel. Ranging in age from thirty to fifty-five, the three men were quietly observing action in the street as they drank their bottles of beer.

Music blared from the car wash across the street. Cars stopped in front of us, and people jumped out to go into the liquor store. Pretty girls walked right past us and the three men didn't notice. They seemed like the people I needed to ask.

"I'm looking for my father. Do you know El Tio?"

"Who are you?"

"I'm Neto. Jesús' son from Mazatlán."

"Sure. I know him," said El Burro. "Sit down. Do you want something?"

My throat was dry and a drink sounded like a good idea. I went inside the liquor store, bought a six-pack of beer for the four of us, and eased myself onto the wall.

"Your father will be here later," El Camelo reported. "Right now, he's probably working in the auto shop, with Iván and Juan."

We shook hands and exchanged stories as I drank a bottle of beer. My father was alive, but I didn't know how badly he was hurt. I wanted to settle myself before seeing him again.

I finished my beer, said goodbye to my new friends, and walked to the auto shop. Cars were up on jacks. Boxes and tools were spread out everywhere. Two men, my father and my cousin Iván, were on a landing, six steps up, overlooking the shop. I climbed the stairs and grabbed my father's arms.

"Papí! There you are! What happened to you? We didn't know where you were."

Papí grabbed me in a hug. He kissed my face and didn't let go of my hand. He laughed and looked at me, just like he always did.

"*M'hijo,* where have you been? I've been waiting here for someone to come and get me."

"I would have come sooner, but I was busy looking for you in Mazatlán."

"That's okay, Neto. I knew it would be you who would come for me."

"Why didn't you call me? I would have come right away?"

"I thought you knew where I was. I couldn't remember how to call you. I was in an accident. I get confused sometimes."

We talked about everything. Papí wanted to know about my mother and my brothers.

"Mamí is in California, working for a couple of Cubans, taking care of their house and their kids. She took Alicia with her, to keep her out of trouble. The boys live in Mazatlán. Rosa and I watch over them, but Rosa has her hands full with her two unruly boys."

Papí looked good to me. He showed me the big gash on his head, the only injury he had from his accident. He didn't remember going over the bridge. He didn't remember who picked him up and took care of him right after the accident. "*M'hijo*, all I know is that she was a kind, gentle woman. I think she was an angel. Or maybe it was the Virgin herself."

Qué milagro! Maybe my father was right. Every morning and every night he prayed to the Virgin, asking her to keep him safe. *How could it be that a woman, a stranger, found him on the road right after the accident? That she took him to her home, kept him for two months, nursed him back to health, and then put him on a bus to Tijuana? And then she disappeared? How could this not be a miracle?*

"Iván," I asked one night when we were drinking, "How did my father get to your place from the bus depot? Did he walk here?"

"No. He showed up in a taxi. He knew I had a repair shop in Cañon Johnson. He told the taxi driver to drive around until he found me."

"Who paid for the taxi?"

"Your father had money in his wallet from before his accident. When he got here, he wasn't like he is now. He was more confused and didn't seem to know where he was. He's gotten better in the past month."

"Why didn't you call me?"

"Hell, Neto. I didn't know how to find you. It's been years since I've seen you, or your mother or your brothers. It's not like I carry your phone number around in my pocket."

"Did he tell you he'd been in an accident?"

"No. Your father didn't mention the accident until I asked him about the scar on his forehead. I was so happy to see him, I thought he just came into town looking for a job. You know, he's forgotten a lot of things but he's still a hell of a mechanic."

• • •

I stayed with my father from March until the end of June. One night there was a rumble in the bar while me and Juan were there, guarding our fathers. The place was packed. Bolas, the guy who owned the muffler shop next to El Padre, was there with his marijuana-using brother, Cuba. Caballo, Burro, and Camelo were there, too, along with some of our friends.

Bolas, a Papago Indian, was a really big guy with a huge heart. He got his name because his stomach stuck out in front of him like a basketball. He looked mean, like a donkey was crossed with a bull, but he was usually hardworking and peaceful.

Bolas and his brother Cuba got in fights every time they were in the bar. There was something about the cantina that made them want to stand up and start swinging.

My father quit drinking as soon as I found him, but he still liked going to the cantina at night after work. That night, Juan and I were sitting at a table with our fathers, laughing and enjoying a beer, when the fight started. Juan and I hustled our fathers out the door, and Juan walked them home.

Jimmy, Juan's little brother, was still in the bar, so I went back to join the fight. By the time I got there, the place was blasting noise. Furniture was tipped over. There must have been at least twenty people punching and shouting curses and spilling blood, and there was a lot of beer all over the floor.

The next thing I knew, sirens were screaming down the street. It took six police cars to break up the fight. They arrested everyone they could, including me and

Jimmy. They put us in El Ocho, the detention center two blocks away. We all slept there until the next morning when we weren't drunk anymore.

El Padre showed up to get us out of jail. "Jimmy, get up. I need you at the shop. Neto, since the two of you are here together, I guess I'll sign you out, too."

• • •

I needed to make some money to pay my expenses. I wanted to work with my father at the auto shop, but Juan didn't need any more help. I decided to start a small business with a guy who called himself Ricky Ricardo, the Coyote Cowboy. We worked together taking people across the border to San Isidro. I charged twenty dollars per person, but if they didn't have that much, I charged them less. Some of the money I kept, and the rest I gave to Ricky.

My job taught me humility and patience. It was like pulling drowning people out of the ocean all over again. I wasn't a hero. I was just doing a job.

Tijuana was full of desperate people needing to get across. *Pobrecitos*—poor people with very sad stories. Refugees from Honduras, Chiapas, Guatemala, and Yucatan, their shoes and clothes almost worn away from walking.

They were mostly men, but some women, and were easy for me to find. They looked lost, standing by the border fence, four blocks from the immigration station. There were holes in the fence, and *migración* didn't fix them, practically inviting me to break the law and get these people to a new life.

I walked slowly and introduced myself. I smiled cautiously and asked them if they needed help. I was careful not to make any sudden movements that could scare them off. I told them they could trust me. I listened carefully as they told me about their lives.

"I'm okay, but my daughter has seizures and we can't afford the medicine. I need to go to the US to work in the fields."

"I'm okay, but my wife is at home taking care of too many children. I'm a tile layer. A good tile layer. I don't make enough money to feed my family. *Mi amigo* told me there is work in California."

"I need to get to San Francisco. My brother called me. My father is dying. I need to see him to say goodbye."

My job was easy. In a quiet voice, I told them I could help them. I told them to meet me back there that night, in the same place by the fence.

By the light of the moon, I gave my customers something to eat and clean clothes to wear. I guided them around the first and second hill and into Ricky's van, where he was waiting under the highway, to drive them to San Isidro.

My life was good. I was shooting pool with my friends, meeting beautiful women, staying away from prostitutes, and making a little money helping people cross the border. Meanwhile, Juan Vargas was having something to do with Veronica, his wife's sister. The only problem was that he was still married to Arianna.

Veronica and I hooked up when Juan took a vacation back to Mazatlán. I decided to move in with her while I was keeping an eye on my father. Veronica went to work every day in the US and brought home a six-pack of Budweiser every night. I wasn't doing any hard drugs, only pot and beer, and Veronica liked me a lot.

Veronica was a beautiful woman with a gorgeous face and sexy body. When Juan came back, she didn't want him anymore. She only wanted me. But Juan was jealous. He found me and threatened to kick my ass. I knew I could beat him up, but it was time for me to go.

"I need to leave. I need to go to the US. My mother is looking for me," I told Veronica. "I wish I could stay, but now that Juan is back, it's not right."

"Don't go. I'm alone here," Veronica pleaded. "Juan is still with Arianna."

"Don't worry. You'll be okay. Juan will take care of you. I promise, I will never forget you."

The same week, two friends from Mazatlán called to see if I could get them across the border. There was a job waiting in Tujunga, in the hills outside of LA.

I put my father on the bus to Mazatlán at the end of June. On July 4, I met my friends. We crossed into

California, going to work for a big printing press in Tujunga Canyon.

Back in Mazatlán, Papí totally turned his life around. He went home to watch over Cachi and Franco. He worked as a security guard and he fixed cars on the street, outside our house. He watched my sister Rosa trying to raise boys by herself and decided to help support them. He was devoted to his grandsons. He never drank again. He continued to kneel before La Virgen de Guadalupe twice a day, to thank her for saving his life, to ask for her protection going forward, and to beg her to watch over the rest of us.

20
Tujunga

The phone rang in Juan's shop. I wiped my greasy hands on my jeans and put down my tools as I picked up the phone.

"Hola, Neto. It's me and Tony," Ruben shouted into the phone.

"*Qué onda, cabron?* Where the hell are you?"

"We're in Mazatlán. We need to find work right away. Chorizo is working at a printing press. He said he can set us up where he works. Can you get us into California?"

"Yeah, sure. I just put my father on the bus. How many people does Chorizo need?"

"He said his boss needs a lot of help. A whole crew. Maybe enough work for all of us."

I'd never thought of working as a printer, but I needed to find something to do. Whatever it was, I knew I could do it. I was ready for a change.

"Where is the printing press?"

"I dunno. Some place called Tujunga. It's in California, I think. Maybe by LA."

"Where's Tony? I want to talk to him."

Tony's loud voice boomed through the telephone. "*Hola, cabron.* Are you going to cross us?"

"*Porque no?* Why not? How soon can you get here?"

"We can be there by the end of the week. We're coming on a bus. How are you going to get us to California?"

"Don't worry. We'll cross the river at night. Bring surfer clothes. Long shorts and bright Hawaiian shirts. We need to look like we belong at the beach. Put all your belongings in a backpack. Call me back when you get to Tijuana."

"Neto, thanks."

"No problem. I am on my way to LA anyway. I need to get out of Tijuana before my cousin chases me with a gun." I smiled into the telephone.

Juan shouted "That's right!" and shook his fist at me.

• • •

We were a rowdy bunch. Young guys from Mazatlán. Soccer players. Heavy drinkers and pot smokers. Leaving the country where we were born to go to work. Looking for girlfriends. Looking for parties. Looking for fun.

Ruben and Tony knew my reputation. We grew up in the same neighborhood and played soccer together when we were kids. Ruben was twenty-five, two years older than me, and Tony was a year younger. They knew I could get them across the border.

We crossed the river in the early morning of July 4, 1983. We wanted to be in California to celebrate the holiday. Ricky Ricardo dropped us off at Playa Tijuana, on the road next to the river.

We crossed at three in the morning. It was an easy crossing. The temperature was warm, with a soft breeze coming from the ocean. Overhead, only a sliver of moon rose up to guide us. Pelicans sailed across the purple sky. Seagulls called to us in screeching voices, as they walked across the sand.

"It's okay," they squawked. "The coast is clear. All the guards have gone home. They're drinking beer. Getting ready for parties and fireworks."

I'd helped others do the crossing so many times, I was sure I could do it. I rehearsed it in my head: *Ask someone to drive us to the car wash. Get out and climb down the rocky cliff. Walk four blocks along the sandbar to a place where we can cross the river. Wade across with our packs on our heads. Carry rags to erase our footprints on the sand. Once we get across, keep walking away from the water. Hustle ourselves to the rocks in front of the penthouses. Hide out in the rocks if there is any noise.*

The only sound I heard was the crashing of waves as they hit the shore. *No migra!*

"Thanks, Neto. That was easier than I thought it would be."

"I told you I knew what I was doing. I could make it across in my sleep." I didn't want my friends to know that every crossing was dangerous. Even trips that seemed easy had their own hidden traps.

We walked along the road together as I scouted our way to the San Isidro trolly. The three of us hopped on the trolly, smiling and laughing our way into San Diego.

Ruben called Toñeras, a friend from Mazatlán, from a pay phone. "We're in town, me and Tony and Neto. We've been up all night and need a place to sleep. Can you come and pick us up?"

"Of course. Where exactly are you?"

"We're in San Diego. At the trolly stop."

"I'll be right there. Ten minutes."

Toñeras left Mazatlán two years before. He was a good guy. Short and strong, he wanted to be a big-time gang member. To be rich and famous. He loved the thrill, the rush that came with big money and living with danger. But when he almost got caught by the police for a famous robbery, he left Mexico and moved to San Diego. His girlfriend was a friend of mine. Toñeras broke her heart when he left without saying goodbye. Not even a hug. He just disappeared. We heard that some people were looking for him even after he went to the live in the US.

"Toñeras, do you like living here?"

"Yeah. It's quiet and that's okay. I like the person that I am here. When I was with the gang, I was pissed off all the time. It got so nothing mattered. I hated everyone. Even my family. I would just as soon kill someone as look at them."

I knew what he meant. I was like that when I came back from Portland. And when I was sent back to Mexico when I was fourteen. I believe that most people have both a good person and a bad person inside them. I was happy to see "the Good Toñeras" again.

"Toñeras, you're a good cook," I said, my mouth stuffed with ribs, salad, mashed potatoes, and corn on the cob.

"Slow down, *pendejo*. You're going to choke."

"You slow down." I grabbed another rib before it disappeared.

The next morning, Ruben called Chorizo. "Hey, does the printing press still need workers?"

"*Si*. We're all working overtime. Can you get to LA? I'll pick you up there. Where will you be?"

"Neto, where can Chorizo pick us up?"

"At my sister's house. Corner of Arborvitae and Glasgow."

"How soon will you get here?"

"Maybe the day after tomorrow."

We argued about how we could get to LA. Could we take a bus? Hitchhike?

"How much does it cost to fly?" Ruben asked Toñeras.

"You can get a one-way ticket for forty-five dollars."

"Look, I have two hundred dollars. I can pay for all of us. You guys can pay me back later," Ruben offered.

"What?" I was outraged. "After I helped you make the crossing, you want me to pay you back to fly to LA? I'll pay you with my fist."

"No problem, Neto. *Cálmate, güey.* I'll pay."

Toñeras dropped us off at the Coronado Bridge. We said goodbye to our friend and never saw or heard from him again. I think we might have been the last people to ever see him alive.

The three of us walked single file for two miles across the bridge, directly to the airport. The bridge is high over the ocean, so high that I couldn't look down without my head starting to swim. I kept my gaze focused on Tony's ass all the way to the airport.

Chorizo borrowed a car from his roommate, Arturo, a mechanic at the printing press. He drove up in Arturo's '66 Mustang and honked the horn three times.

"Thanks, Alicia," we yelled to my sister. We grabbed our backpacks, put on our baseball caps, and scrambled out the door. "*Gracias por todo.*"

We tried to be cool, but we were all grinning as we jostled our way down the sidewalk. We were ready for a new life in this new land.

"Ok, *cabrones*. Are you ready to go to work?"

"Good to see you, Chorizo. *Vamanos!*"

We piled into the car and rode thirty-five miles up the *cañon* to Tujunga. Dry air mixed with the smell of exhaust from Arturo's car. The metallic blue Mustang climbed higher, the path curving around rocky ledges and short, scruffy trees. Cool breezes, the smell of wild grass and yucca, piñon and pine trees. Wildflowers on the side of the road, the mountains in the distance—this place was a new beginning for me. No longer hot and humid, like Mazatlán, or even LA. No palm trees or mango groves. Instead, clear fresh air blowing across my face and through my hair. Soft clouds danced high up in the sky. A lizard sat like a king on a rock, warming his skin in the sun. *Are there rattlesnakes here?* I wondered. *Is there anything to watch out for?*

"Chorizo, what is this place we're going to?" Ruben wanted to know.

"It's Sunland-Tujunga. I don't know why it got that name. See the mountains right there? Those are the San Gabriels. Right now, we're in the Verdugo foothills."

"Is it always cooler here than in LA?"

"Yeah, mostly. We're leaving the ocean and climbing into the hills. It's a lot drier here. The rain is softer. The people are kinder. It's a nice place to live."

I looked back, out the rear window. Tujunga reminded me of Portland. All those evergreen trees. I hoped that wasn't a bad omen.

Monday morning, we went straight to work. We were pressmen, the Mazatlán crew, working for the Sunland-Tujunga Record Ledger. Nobody cared about legal papers, only if we could do the work. We had a job. We had each other. We just needed to find a place to live.

Chorizo and Arturo already had an apartment. They lived on Foothill Boulevard, four blocks up the hill from the Record Ledger. Tony, Ruben, and I rented an apartment close by. Our landlord was a friendly, happy Armenian guy with a grouchy, skinny wife. He smiled a lot and she never did. All of us were taller than they were.

The Sunland-Tujunga press was a family business. Ellie and her husband, Joe, shook our hands and told us they were happy to have us working for them. We stood around, with our hands in our pockets, looking like happy little boys.

"We're happy to be here, too," Tony, Chorizo, and I mumbled together.

Ruben turned to us. "*Qué dice?*" he wanted to know. "What did she say?"

"She said that she likes us and that we are all very handsome," I told him. "Now we need to get to work."

Ellie was a pretty woman who wore dresses every day, even in the cold season. Her blue eyes crinkled when she talked to us. She was passionate about the printing business, always encouraging us to work hard, to do our best, to be better than we were.

Ellie introduced us to Keith Parker, the boss over the entire operation. "Okay, guys, this is Keith. His job is to teach you to be pressmen. To keep you in line and keep you safe." We bobbed our heads. "He's going to make sure everything gets out the door on time."

Keith was quiet, a little shy even. He nodded and ran his fingers through his long brown hair as we told him our names.

"Hey, I'm glad you guys are here. We run two shifts here and I'm short of workers. Each shift is ten hours plus two hours overtime every day. Chorizo, tell these guys how busy we are."

"The press runs like a fast-track train, all day and all night. We print two hundred different magazines and flyers every week. Every week we put out two newspapers: *The Star* and the *Globe*. We have one big press that can handle as many as six rolls of paper when we're at max. Most of the time, we run three rolls of paper and have three cylinders empty, waiting for the next job."

"That's a lot of pages."

"Yeah. When we're at full capacity, we print ten thousand copies every hour."

"I've got some crews already set up. Some of the guys, like Chorizo, have been here a long time. I need you guys to fill in the gaps. I know you are friends, but I need to break you up, to add you to the crews we've already got going."

That was fine with us. We saw enough of each other anyway. And we needed to work different shifts so could trade spaces to sleep.

When Ganso, another friend from Mazatlán, came to Tujunga two weeks later, we needed to shift roommates. Ganso moved in with me and Tony. Ruben moved in with Chorizo. And Arturo decided to live by himself in the Little Tijuana Apartments.

Our place was just a small wooden shack, with cobwebs in the corners and old linoleum on the floor. There wasn't much room to move around. Two sofas and inflatable beds took up the whole place. We had a refrigerator, a table with four chairs and a stove in the kitchen. Next to the bathroom was a big closet with hangers for all our clothes. There weren't any dressers or shelves, but it was okay. We didn't have a lot of clothes.

Sometimes we had extra people sleeping there. Friends who came to drink and fell asleep before they could go home. Sometimes there were six people sleeping at our place, three at night and three in the morning.

"I need to charge you Mexicans extra for letting your friends sleep here. This is too many people," the Armenian woman would grumble.

"No, we work different shifts. We sleep when we aren't working, so we aren't using any electricity or gas. Actually, we're saving you money." I reasoned.

November, the weather started to change. Cold,

dry wind blew through our shack. We put on layers of clothes, but we were still cold.

"You can have this little heater," our landlady barked, "but make sure you keep it away from your clothes. Do you understand? I don't want you getting drunk and burning this place down."

"Yes, ma'am."

"And make sure you smoke outside."

There were days I showed up to work, tired and hungover from the night before. It didn't matter. I wanted to prove myself to Ellie. To be the best worker she'd ever had.

"*Buenos dias, señora.* How are you today?" My teeth shined my biggest smile, and I twinkled my eyes at her.

Ellie shook her head and smiled at my attempts at Mexican charm. "You Mazatlán guys are good. Our success is all because of you. I can't do without you."

Ellie and Joe had two beautiful daughters, not much older than us, who answered the phones. They wore lipstick every day and mascara on their long, curvy eyelashes. We wanted to impress them, too, but we were always respectful. They saw us at our best and we wanted to keep it that way.

Soon Keith realized that paying overtime was costing too much money. "You guys are good workers, but the overtime pay is killing us. From now on we're running three shifts. Neto and Chorizo, I'm promoting you to assistant operators. Here's how it's going to be: Shift one will work from six in the morning until two in the afternoon. I'll come in early and get us started. Chorizo and Ganso will help me.

"Shift two will work from two until ten. Neto, you will be in charge of that shift. I'll be around to help you. Ruben and Pancho, who grew up in California, will work with you. Is that okay with you?"

"Yes, sir."

Pancho didn't live with us, but he was Mexican and fit right in. He came to our place almost every day after work, to kick back and get drunk before going home for the night.

"Shift three is the night shift. They'll work from ten o'clock to six in the morning. Catalino will be in charge. Tony will work that shift with Emiliano, Catalino's friend from Michoacan."

We were hard workers. We wore hats to keep our long hair out of the presses. The machines never stopped. Noise was everywhere. It bounced off the walls and vibrated through our bodies. More noise than a rock band in a small nightclub.

This was a different kind of noise. A mechanical, constant *ka-chung* as the rolls of paper spun through the presses. We couldn't talk. I couldn't hear myself think, so I stopped thinking and just reacted.

We changed the paper rolls fast. They were heavy but we were strong. As an assistant operator, my job was to add color cassettes to the rolls. I had to be fast. I couldn't stop the presses running. I constantly checked the metal lines that held the paper rolls in place to make sure nothing was loose.

Usually when the printing was finished, huge rolls of now-printed paper were cut and put together so that the pages fell in the correct order. The product was then ready to be shipped to the end destination.

Meanwhile, other pressmen were changing paper to fit the work order. There were different thicknesses and qualities of paper, some shiny photo paper and some cheap thin paper, depending on the job. The ink smell mixed with our sweat as we jumped like cats from job to job. Our mission was clear: Keep the machines running. As the papers came spitting out of the presses in a tight pile, big sewing machines tied the bundles with a leash and dropped them onto pallets. We used our feet to run the sewing machines and our hands to make sure the bundles were secure. They needed to fit precisely on the pallet, ready to go downstairs to the shipping room.

We printed newspapers, TV guides, supermarket ads, and magazines—*National Enquirer* and *The Star*. I liked reading the gossip magazines before they were delivered. I read every morning before my shift started. We all did. The Mazatlán crew was more updated on Hollywood gossip than almost anyone, anywhere. I knew who was getting married, who was arrested, and who had been spotted in a night club with someone he shouldn't have been with. The magazines taught me to read and talk like a gringo.

I earned $7.50 an hour. Almost $300 by the end of the week. The lady at the liquor store cashed my paycheck for a fee. She knew all of us by name because we stopped in there every night to buy beer and tequila. I also used my money to buy food, cigarettes, Coca-Cola, and weed.

In some ways, being a pressman was like working on the shrimp boats. The shrimp boats were more dangerous, but being a pressman was just as relentless. Both jobs were sophisticated in their own way. When we came to work, it was "all hands on deck." No one could stop or call a time-out. The shrimp needed to be harvested and the presses couldn't stop. Both jobs were joyful. I liked working with guys who knew how to do the job and did it well. Once I got used to it, being a pressman was easy. I could have done it forever.

• • •

By July, I had worked for Ellie and Joe a whole year. I was happy living in the *cañon* and being a pressman. I had a sweet girlfriend, surfing friends in Redondo, and soccer buddies in Glendale. I knew my way around Los Angeles, and I was making money on the side. Everything was good until Ruben did a really stupid thing that ruined everything.

We worked that Saturday because the press was especially busy. Ruben was drinking on the job. I knew he was drinking, but I didn't care. I went home after my shift, smoked a joint, and fell asleep. Ruben went home and kept drinking with Chorizo until they both passed out. When he woke up in the morning, he was still drunk.

If I had kicked his ass right then, I might still be a pressman today. Instead, I went back to sleep and Ruben went to the printing press, where he found the keys to the big delivery truck. He went home and picked up Chorizo. Together, they drove to our house and convinced Ganso to come along. Ruben wanted me and Tony, too.

"No, you drunken fool. I'm not going with you, and you leave Tony alone, too. I don't like taking things that aren't mine. I'll kick your ass if you pick up Tony." He knew I meant it.

Ruben, Ganso, and Chorizo went for a wild ride on that beautiful Sunday morning, Three *barrachos* in the big delivery truck, bouncing and weaving their way up the *cañon*. They were easily spotted, and someone called the owners.

Keith Parker knew right away something was wrong when he saw that the truck was gone. He knocked on Ellie's door. Together, they reported the truck stolen. The fools were stopped by the police up in the mountains. Ganso had twenty joints of weed in his cigarette package. They were all busted.

Tony and I were still asleep when Ellie knocked on our door. She pulled her hair back, put her hands on her forehead, and shook her head slowly from side to side. I knew she smelled weed on our clothes from the night before. Her cheeks were red when she asked me what I knew about the truck being missing.

"Ellie, you have to believe me." I felt like I was going to be sick. A sour taste flooded the back of my throat. I swallowed it back down rather than spit in front of Ellie.

"I worked until ten, and Antonio just got off at six. We didn't have anything to do with this. I would never do anything that stupid. I like working here, and so does Tony. Ruben came looking for us, but I told him to leave us alone. I told him I'd kick his ass if he took Tony with him."

My shoulders sagged with the weight of what had just happened. Ruben and Chorizo stole the truck from Ellie, but they stole from me and Tony, too. They stole Ellie's trust and respect from us that morning. They took away our future. Our lives took a wrong turn as the truck was weaving its way around the hills of Tujunga. I don't know if I could have stopped them. With all my heart, I wish I had tried.

Ellie shook her head and didn't take her eyes off me. She looked right into my soul. We were both sad, knowing that this moment couldn't be relived. Ellie knew what she had to do. I did, too. I knew I couldn't stay.

Ruben, Chorizo, and Ganso got fired. They hung around Tujunga but didn't have any work to do. The whole town knew what they had done, and no one would hire them. Our Armenian landlord was after us all the time to pay the rent, but we couldn't afford it without Ganso paying his share.

Me and Tony grew tired of dragging around those freeloaders, and I didn't want to look at them anymore. Ellie hired new pressmen from California, but the fun had gone out of the job. I started to miss the carefree life of the ocean. The days were long. People on the street started looking at us like we, too, had done something wrong. Tony and I worked at the printing press for another four months, until November 1984, when we quit and moved to LA.

Chorizo was a good sponsor for us, but he went downhill after stealing the truck. He had it made at the printing press. He'd been there for two years before we got there. He had a nice girlfriend, who had a lot of money and owned her own house. They threw parties with pot and beer and had good times together. I think Dora loved Chorizo, even though he was always scamming her. They stayed together until Chorizo got himself deported and moved back to Mazatlán.

Twenty-five years later, Chorizo was fifty years old and living in Mazatlán when his liver blew up and he died. Tony killed himself, at home in Mazatlán, the next year. I still see Ganso and Ruben sometimes, on the streets of Mazatlán, but I don't talk to them. Whenever I remember what they did to me in Tujunga, I turn and walk away.

21
Maria

Tujunga, part of the Simi and San Fernando valleys, was even colder than Portland. By January we were running our heater all day. Most of the guys had never seen ice or snow before.

"Damn, Chorizo, you should have warned us about the cold. I'm missing Mazatlán a lot right now."

"Of course, it's cold, *estupido*. You're in the mountains. Enjoy it. It'll be spring soon enough."

Sundays, when I wasn't at the beach, me and Ruben played soccer in Glendale, a suburb about fifteen miles away. Vincente, a housepainter during the week, played with us and gave us a ride down the valley.

We were all good soccer players, enjoying the game just for fun. I still had my left-foot technique that I learned as a kid, but now I was bigger and stronger, and my reactions were faster. It wasn't long before a bunch of Armenians noticed us. Vincente introduced us to these guys from Russia.

"We saw you play. You guys are good. Come over and play with us. You can help us win," they said in strong Russian accents.

The Armenians played rough. They threw elbows and kicks. Every game was a brawl. We had to be crazy to join them, but they paid each of us seventy dollars for the afternoon. We played with one team for half a game and then switched places and played with another team for half.

This is the way my life was supposed to be. I'd been in Tujunga for eight months, working hard at the printing press, playing soccer with Vincente and the Armenians on weekends, and going to Redondo Beach once a month to surf and party with my friends from Mazatlán.

The bus to Redonda was ninety minutes each way. Paco, part of the original Olas Altas Crew, was there working for Donato's construction company. Lobo showed up sometimes, too. It was fun to talk about Mazatlán and the people we used to know. I always asked about Checo and Nolas, but no one seemed to know where they were, or if they still loved surfing as much as I did.

Paco lived with Mateo, a guy from Redondo, in a nice house we called the Animal House. It was a place to lay back, with three bedrooms and a shack in the back for storing surfboards. We could bring girls there if we wanted to. Or meet up with girls we'd just met on the beach.

I liked to party in the Animal House, but when it came time to sleep, I preferred the shack, with its tall ceiling and windows all the way to the back. Sleeping there was like sleeping in an attic. I was the guardian of the boards and far enough away from the noise of the main house. The distant sound of cold waves pounding against rocks sang me to sleep.

Redondo felt like a second home. It reminded me of the years I lived on Stone Island, when Donato was our big brother and Paco and I were part of the pack. My life opened up as soon as I stepped off the bus and took a deep breath of salty air. My face, dry as a pine tree from living in the *cañon*, soaked up every drop of welcome moisture. I had missed being near the ocean. I was eager to grab a board and get in the waves.

Surfing has always been the way I make peace in my world. It is my salvation. My church. My religion. No matter how many people are bobbing in the water, I am happy to be among them. I smile and say hello, but then I swim away, more comfortable riding alone. I listen for the waves and wait for them to call my name. I am always the brave one. The one who jumps first, leaving the others behind me. The one who doesn't back down when I sense a huge shoulder rearing up behind me.

I am both powerful and calm as I jump on my board. My feet are cold from the water, while the sun beats down on my head. I want to escape the life of the city and explore the water, swimming with sea animals. Staying under water for as long as I can before coming up for air.

Riding a wave, every fiber of my body is alert. There is just me and the fiberglass underneath as I shuffle my feet, finding my place between the sea and the sky. I focus on the water ahead of me, looking for danger, watching for shallow water and rocks. Meanwhile, my body reacts without thinking to currents pushing me from behind, keeping me steady. I look for opportunities to turn into the swells, to dance with the energy of the waves beneath me, to glide into the barrels and come out the other side. Happiness floods my whole being. This is where I am meant to be.

Paco and Mateo worked hard building houses during the week. On payday, they bought kegs of beer. Friends came from up and down the coast to meet and party together. All weekend, we surfed and laughed about the old times, got drunk, and grilled fish and *carne asada* outside. It was a good life. All I still needed was a steady girlfriend.

• • •

"Who is that pretty girl across the street?" I asked Vincente one day. We were drinking beer after getting our asses kicked by the Armenians in the weekly soccer game. I groaned every time I moved.

"I don't really know her, but I think she's looking at you."

I felt a thump in my chest. I felt a tingle down below. I was excited in a way I hadn't been for a long time. I want to yell, "Hello. Who are you?" but my mouth was suddenly dry as a yucca. I coughed to clear my throat. *Maybe Vincente was right? I would be a fool not to say hello.*

Maria swayed in a blue rocking chair on her porch. She didn't move from her spot in the shade when I shouted across the street.

"Hi. Is this where you live?" I called to her in English.

"Come over and talk to me."

I grabbed my skateboard and was at her gate before she could blink her pretty eyes. My bruised body was healed by this angel with long black hair.

"Who are you? I can see that you aren't shy or afraid."

Maria was an American Indian but with blue eyes, the color of the ocean on a cold, cloudy day. She was tall, almost as tall as me, and her hair fell halfway down her back.

"Not when I see a pretty girl, I'm not shy."

"Where are you from?"

"Sinaloa, Mexico. Have you heard of it?"

"Not really. I know Mexico, but not Sinaloa."

"Where are you from, *chula*?"

"I'm from Oregon. Come inside. I like you already. You have the happy smile of a pure Indian guy."

From that day on, Maria was my precious girl-friend. It was a time of free love and clean sex. We were committed to each other and always used pro-tection. We held on to each other and didn't argue. I didn't have any other girlfriends when I was with Ma-ria. For the next eight months, she was my everything.

Maria had a little boy, Bobby, about three years old. Her house was small and clean, with one bed-room and a large living room for watching TV. Her yard circled the house with flowers. I visited Maria on weekends and sometimes in the morning before I started my shift. I liked her son, but I didn't see a lot of him. Maria wanted to protect him from seeing us together.

"Sweetheart, I don't want my son to get to know you. He will only be disappointed when it's time for you to leave."

"But maybe I don't have to leave. I'm happy here. Can't I stay?"

"You can stay as long as you like. But someday you will leave. I already know that."

When I came to the door, Maria sent Bobby to stay with the family next door. Sheila and Shelly, his babysitters, were like family to Maria. The girls were in ninth grade and very responsible. They were pretty American girls with blond hair that hung past their shoulders. The girls were good skaters, tomboys with long, strong legs.

The girls played with Bobby and watched out for him They watched out for Maria, too. She was a sweet woman with a serious drug problem. Even I knew that. Maria liked weed a little. She liked angel dust a lot more.

Maria's house was a meeting point for her friends, mostly bikers and heavy drug users. I didn't like them. They bothered me as they roared their Harleys and Yamahas down the *cañon* and up the street, kicking up dust, disturbing my peace.

"Maria, why do you hang around these guys? I don't like them. They look at me like they are jealous. I don't trust them."

"No, Neto, they aren't going to hurt you. They are my customers."

"What customers? What are you selling?"

"They buy heroin from me. Usually they give me money, but sometimes I get PCP from them instead."

"I don't like the sound of that."

"It's okay. Don't worry. I think you can help me, if you want to."

That's how Maria and I went into business together. Every fifteen days, I bought heroin from a dealer for $1,500 and sold it to Maria for the same amount. She turned around and sold it to the bikers for $3,000. She kept $1,000 and gave me $500. I used that money to go to Redondo. On my way home from Redondo, I'd stop and pick up more drugs to take back to Maria. Sometimes I'd stop to see my mother and give her a little money.

"If this is drug money, I don't want it."

"No, Mamí. This is the money I earn at the newspaper."

I wanted Maria to stop using PCP, but she loved getting high. I didn't want to try it. I hated that Maria used it so much.

"I don't trust that stuff, Maria. You never know what's going to happen."

One day, Sheila and Shelly ran down the street to find me. I was at Vincente's house when I heard them call my name. They were out of breath and sweaty when I came outside.

"*M'hijas*. What's the matter? Is it Maria? Has something happened to Bobby?"

"Quick, Neto. Maria sent us. She told us to find you. She needs you right now."

I sprinted to her house, slamming the door behind me. Maria was lying on the sofa, as peaceful as an angel. I bent down to smell her breath, to make sure she was alive. I kissed her and sang to her as I stroked her beautiful hair.

"Papí's here. It's okay. Don't worry. Papí's here," I murmured in her ear. I sat her up and stayed until she was awake, my arms circling her as she laid her forehead on my chest.

"Thank goodness you came back, my love. You scared me this time. Why do you have to keep doing this?"

"Neto, you should try it. At least once. It will put you in a trance. You watch yourself float up to the ceiling and around the room. Looking down on the world and feeling at peace. You will drift like you are swimming on your back in the ocean."

"Okay. But only once. If I don't like it, I'm never using it again."

Maria gave me some to try at home, away from her and Bobby. I dipped the tip of my cigarette in PCP and took a couple of drags. It was pure PCP. I went crazy. My skin was on fire.

"Shower! Shower! I need a shower. Put some soap on me. Get this off my skin." I was screaming, but no one could hear me. The words were slamming into each other inside my head.

My body surged with the strength of an elephant. I picked up the sliding glass door that was on the shower, took it off the track, and put it in the hallway. I knew I was dying until I stood, naked under a stream of cold water. I didn't come out until the drug wore off. My chest was heaving from exertion. My eyes watered from the cold.

I went back to Maria's the next day. "I hate that stuff you gave me. It put me on fire. I was Superman and I didn't like it."

"Oh, I'm sorry. I didn't tell you. You can't use it with

your usual cigarettes. You need to cut it with menthol. You need to use Super Kool menthols. Regular cigarettes are too strong."

I never used PCP again. I kept buying PCP juice from my supplier to sell to the bikers with the heroin they wanted. I bought a little bottle for $150 and sold it to the bikers for $300. After Chorizo and Ruben got fired, I used drug money to pay the rent. But I always sold PCP with a pack of Super Kools. Even if I didn't like those guys, I needed to protect my customers. If they got aggressive, they could kill someone.

Maria was right. I wasn't destined to stay in Tujunga forever. I was twenty-four years old, with my life ahead of me. For a while I thought I might become a pressman and live in the *cañon* with Maria for the rest of my life, but my life changed the minute Ruben stole the truck. I was selling drugs to pay for a small, crappy apartment far away from the ocean. I no longer loved my newspaper job. I needed to say goodbye to Tujunga and to my sweet Maria. I walked away with my chin up, shaking my head to hide tears in my eyes.

Tajunga taught me to enjoy being in the US, surrounded by people I loved. I learned to speak English. I learned I was meant to work and be happy, to have friends and lovers. To be helpful and appreciated. For a short time, I moved to Redondo to live in The Animal House. America was my home now. It was a long time before I went back to live in Mexico.

22

Maya

I left my job at the printing press and came back to LA. With no money in my pocket and no place to live, I moved in with my sister Alicia. I missed Maria but knew it wouldn't be long before I found another girlfriend.

I'd been watching Maya for a week before she stopped me on my way to the store. She was sitting low in her car, waiting for me to ride by on my skateboard. She wriggled her finger at me, motioning me to her window.

"Hi! Who are you? I've seen you riding around my house. Where are you going?"

"I'm going to the store to get a salad for my sister. Can I get you something?"

"I don't need anything right now. Get in, there's something I want to tell you."

I got in. I didn't know her. I was suspicious, but she was a pretty girl. I wanted to know more.

"I want you to come to my birthday party."

"Sure. When is your party?"

"Tonight. I'm Maya. I'm turning twenty-five."

"Sure, Maya. I'm Neto. Happy birthday."

I asked her, right out, "Are you a cop? You look like a cop." The truth is Maya didn't look any more like a cop than most people. But I was using hard drugs, so I woke up suspicious of everybody.

"No, I'm not a cop. Why?"

"It's the way you talk, with your chin lifted, and moving your shoulders from side to side. Why don't you take off your sunglasses?"

Maya left her sunglasses on. She lifted her short dress and flashed me. My mouth fell open. I blinked twice to make sure that I was seeing right. Maya wasn't wearing any panties. She let me get a good look.

"Now do you think I look like a cop?"

Maya was born in the US. Her mother was from Cuba. Her father was from Yucatan. She looked like an American Indian with slanted eyes. She was short and trim, with long, straight black hair, always pulled back from her forehead with a leather headband.

"I'll come to your party, but I don't have a present for you."

"You will be my present. You don't need to give me anything else."

I was grinning by the time I got back home with Alicia's salad.

I called a friend. "Hey, Rafi, can I borrow your car? I'm going to a party. I want to look good."

I couldn't sit still as I waited for the clock to tell me it was time to leave. I was laughing and babbling to myself as I got dressed and walked out the door.

"Wow, Neto, this is a beautiful car. Is it yours?"

"Not really. I borrowed it. But it's mine for tonight."

Maya grabbed my hand and we walked through the door. I adjusted my shorts as we walked inside. The music was loud, the room filled with people I'd never seen before.

"Hey, Maya, who are these people? I'm the only one here who isn't Black. These guys look like gang members. Should I be afraid?"

"No, they are my friends. Come on. Let's dance."

"Okay. But these people make me nervous."

"Don't you have any drugs?"

"I have about twenty quaaludes in my pocket. They're not for sale, but I can give you some for your birthday."

"Then let's go to my room."

We went to Maya's room and didn't come out. People were dancing and laughing and drinking right outside the room. They pounded on the door. But Maya and I were getting to know each other, and we didn't come out.

Maya and I settled in and spent most of our time together after her birthday. She was the excitement

I needed to forget Maria and my life in Tujunga. I found a job working for Daylight Freight Systems as a delivery person.

Alicia was a good sister to let me stay with her, but I needed a more permanent place to live. She and her boyfriend were talking about getting married. I didn't want to be in the way.

"Neto, you can live here with me and my girls if you help me pay the rent," Maya said one day.

That's how it started. Maya and I lived together for a year and a half. Even though I wasn't always a faithful boyfriend, I loved Maya.

Maya had two daughters. Teresa was nine, and Tania was four. Tania's father was in jail in Chino, California, for being drunk and disorderly. Maya divorced him, but she still went to visit him once a week, until he got out of jail two months after I met her.

Teresa's father was an old man, as old as Maya's father.

"Maya, how did you end up getting pregnant by such an old man."

"I don't know, Neto. I started doing drugs when I was fourteen. I was having sex with men for money. And then I got pregnant."

"Did your parents know what was going on?"

"I don't think my father did, but I'm pretty sure my mother knew. I used to give her some of the money I made." Tears welled in her eyes. "I'm not proud of what I did."

• • •

Maya's parents owned three apartments, side by side, on a hillside in Inglewood, California. We lived in one apartment, and Maya's sister Sophia lived next door. Sophia's chihuahua, Cookie, used to sneak into our house at night. That dog was *El Diablo*—always barking and growling, showing his teeth, and lunging at me. Cookie tried to bite me every time I came in the room. I was afraid of that horrible tiny dog and I didn't want him in our apartment.

One night, I got sick on heroin. It was some really bad stuff. I was sweating, and every inch of me hurt. My bones. My head. Everything was on fire. I thought I might die.

"Neto, I'm afraid. You're sweating and delirious. You're not making any sense. You need to go to the hospital."

"No, don't take me to the hospital. I'll get arrested."

"Then try to drink some water."

"No, I'm not drinking any water. I can't take a piss because it hurts too much."

That night, after I passed out, Cookie snuck to our apartment, looking for trouble. He crawled onto the bed between me and Maya while I was still delirious. In the middle of a nightmare, I rolled over and smothered the stupid dog. The next morning, Sophia let herself into our house, calling for Cookie.

"Cookie? Cookie, baby, where are you?"

Maya came out of our room holding the dead dog in her arms. Sophia went crazy. She stormed into our room and started beating on me with her fists.

"You killed my dog! You filthy Mexican. You killed Cookie!"

"Why didn't you keep your ugly dog at home?"

"You hated my dog. I know you killed him on purpose."

"You're half right. I hated Cookie, but I didn't try to kill him. I must have rolled over in my sleep."

"I'm calling the police."

"Because your dog is dead?"

"Because you killed him."

The police came and made a report. I was not arrested, but that incident is still on my police record today. As soon as the dog died, the fever left me and I was okay. But that stupid dog is still chasing me.

After the dog died, Maya's mother came to talk to us. "Listen, Neto," she said. "You and Maya need to find another place to live. You can't be here near Sophia. She's too upset. Your being here is only going to cause trouble."

"What about the girls? They have friends here. And their school."

"You can leave the girls here with us. You and Maya need to find a different place."

Maya was happy to move. She was going to El Camino Community College to learn to be a nurse, and she wanted to be close to her new friends. Her friends lived in fancy places like Long Beach and Palos Verdes. Maya wanted to be part of that life. She wanted to be rich, and I wanted to make her happy.

We found a place in Lawndale, but it was expensive. Maya loved that huge, modern house with its big patio. I needed to come up with a lot of money for the rent, $700 a month. I knew only one way to make a lot of money in a hurry. I needed to go back to selling drugs.

I got an offer to make $500 in less than three days selling heroin. I didn't even stop to think about it. Maya knew I was dealing drugs, but she didn't care. I didn't tell her that I left my job at Daylight Freight to become a full-time dealer. I stashed my drugs near the airport, in a garage at Alicia's apartment, and started dealing heroin and quaaludes on the street corners in Inglewood.

I was a good drug dealer. I enjoyed the thrill of getting away with something as much as I liked the money I made. I used my skateboard and backpack to move drugs easily from place to place and became the master of disguises. I kept changes of clothes in my backpack. When I thought I was being followed, I slipped into a bathroom. Sometimes I ducked into the bushes and pulled out different clothes. I tried on different hats. Sometimes I hid my skateboard and walked down the street, whistling or singing along with my Walkman.

I was twenty-three years old. Sometimes I tried

to look younger. Sometimes I looked older. Trying to get away from the police was a game of cat and mouse for me. I played it well. Once I even went so far as changing the tattoo on my arm to escape the police. Originally, I had the Olas Altas hill tattooed on my left bicep. The police hassled me. "Look, we know who you are. You're the surfer with the hill tagged on your arm."

So I changed the hill into a pyramid. "No, I'm not the guy you are looking for. See? I have a pyramid on my arm. I'm really an Egyptian."

I was using Mandrax, a powerful quaalude, to keep me from being too hyper, and my heroin habit only got worse. I loved the thrill of taking a hit. After the time I almost overdosed and killed Cookie instead, I was careful to cut my heroin with acetone to lower the strength to ninety-two percent. I asked a Guatemalan guy to show me how to do it. I tried my heroin myself before I sold it. I didn't want what happened to me to happen to my customers.

Twice we moved to other places, eventually ending up in Echo Park. Maya's girls were with us during the week, but on weekends we left the girls with her mother so Maya could party with her new, rich friends. They invited me to their pool parties, but I preferred to go to Redondo to surf or to Inglewood to see my mother.

My mother was always happy to see me. I stopped

first at the *totillaria* or the *frutaria* so I wouldn't show up empty-handed. I wanted her to know I was doing well. But I was careful not to let her know how much money I had or how I made my money.

Mamí liked this new life. California felt like Mazatlán. People spoke Spanish on streets lined with palm trees. The smell of chiles, cooking in oil, and meat roasted on backyard grills, greeted her as she came home from work. She joined a Catholic church in Inglewood and made a lot of new friends. When Padre Alvarez announced he was sponsoring a trip to the Vatican, Mamí was the first person to sign on. She was fifty-seven years old, almost as old as I am now. She came back with stories of everything she had seen and done.

For a working woman from Hacienda del Tamarindo to go to Rome and see the Pope was unheard of. "Neto, that airplane was three blocks long," she reported. She slowly shook her head, as if she couldn't believe it herself. "We walked all day. Some people got tired but not me. I could have walked all day and still walked home at night."

• • •

When I wasn't surfing or visiting my mother, I liked hanging out with Seamus Kelly near Hollywood Park. Seamus was a Vietnam vet, about fifteen years older than me. He knew I was using heroin, but he didn't hassle me about it. Seamus didn't use drugs at all, only alcohol, and not even too much of that.

I liked hanging around Seamus' yard, helping him fix cars. He had a truck that he used to shuttle poor people around. A lot of people came to him for help hauling stuff and for rides. I really liked that about him. His stories of the war fascinated me.

"Seamus, tell me about the war."

"I really don't like talking about it. I thought I was doing the right thing when I signed up, but I saw too many people get messed up."

"Is that why you help a lot of people now?"

"Yeah. Maybe. Friends died right in front of me. There was nothing I could do to save them. Now I do what I can."

In a world full of drug dealers and junkies, including myself, Seamus was a bright light. A true friend. A good human being.

One day, after I finished selling on the street, I started shooting heroin with my friend, Moreno, outside a house where Seamus was drinking with his friends. I started shooting up about four and kept injecting myself every few hours. At eleven, I blacked out and fell flat on the ground. Only by the grace of God was I able to protect my head from bouncing on the curb. Moreno ran inside the house to find Seamus.

"Come outside," Moreno yelled when he spotted

Seamus drinking whiskey in the noisy room. "We've got to get Neto to the hospital. He's unconscious."

My two friends threw me in back of Seamus' truck like a sack of potatoes. Seamus ran two red lights, speeding through the streets of LA in late-night traffic to the nearest hospital.

Morena told me later that Seamus prayed all the way to the hospital. "He's got to live. I can't leave one more friend behind."

I woke up in the hospital. I didn't want to be there, but I was on an IV. I was trapped. I had drugs in my pockets—a chunk of heroin and a package of spoons and matches.

Seamus sat next to me, slumped in a chair by my bed. His eyes looked red and tired as he stared at his empty hands. The wall of machines next to me beeped the slow, steady rhythm of my heart.

"Seamus, you need to go home. Please. Take my drugs. Disappear and take care of my stuff. I'll see you soon."

"I don't want to leave until I know you are okay."

"I'm not gonna die. But I need this shit out of my room before the nurse gets back. Please." Seamus emptied my pockets and walked out. I heard his slow, heavy footsteps open the solid metal door to the hallway and walk away.

By five thirty, I knew I had to get out of there. A big man-nurse came in to take out my IV. He looked like an athlete. I was afraid he could tell I was an addict, and that I was about to fix myself with another dose any minute. I didn't want him to stop me. I waited for him to turn his back and I walked out of the hospital. I was blurry and unsteady, but I had to get away.

Walking down Manchester Street in downtown Inglewood, I saw my old friend, Antonio, coming toward me. I had two spoons in my pocket that I wanted to get rid of.

"Hey, Tony."

"Where're you going?"

"I'm going to see Seamus. Here I don't want these." I pulled the spoons out of my pocket and gave them to Tony and kept walking.

It was daylight when I showed up at Seamus' house. He met me in the alley with a big smile and a hug. He patted me hard on the back.

"God, it's good to see you. I thought you were going to die."

"I might have, amigo. Thank you for last night." Together we walked to his back door.

"Come on in. You made it. I'll make you some breakfast. Do you want to take a shower? You have to be careful from now on."

I kept dealing. It was my way of life. It looked like nothing was going to save me.

23

Emily

Emily Gardner, from Segundo, Georgia, was my side-kick. My buddy. My sometimes girlfriend. Probably my only real love. She brought freedom and joy into my life. She will always be in my heart.

Emily was tall and blond, an athletic gringa. Not glamorous like a movie star, but very pretty. She had a trim, tan body from always being outside. Her blond hair hung past her shoulders. She didn't like to mess with makeup or put her hair in a ponytail. Her *chichis* were small and flat. She said she liked them that way.

I was starting to be uncomfortable around Maya. Her family didn't like me, and my Redondo friends kept telling me to be careful. I felt pressured to sell enough drugs to pay the rent and give Maya money for fancy clothes and shoes. I began to like the thrill of selling drugs on the street, but in the back of my mind I knew what I was doing was wrong.

Emily was different from Maya. Everyone loved her. When she smiled, her bright white teeth made the whole room sparkle. When she met someone new, she asked questions to get to know them better. Her laugh was high, sweet music. Her brown eyes glowed with happiness. Younger than me, but in some ways older, Emily made friends with all the girls in Redondo.

I met Emily at Shakey's Pizza in Inglewood, near Highway 40, where she was the cashier. Maya and I often went to Shakey's to eat pizza, drink pitchers of beer, and hang out with our friends. Musicians, dressed in red-and-white striped shirts and with straw hats on their heads, played loud happy music. People bounced their feet, dancing in their chairs, spilling beer in time to the music.

I noticed Emily right away, and soon Emily's friends were our friends, too. I liked hanging out with the younger kids, especially Emily's younger brother, Ronnie. The legal drinking age in California was twenty-one, but I didn't mind buying pitchers of beer for Ronnie and his friends, just like the Portland guys did for me before I was legal.

I felt carefree when I was with Emily and her friends, not like the heavy feeling I had when I was with Maya. These kids were active and athletic and into skateboarding. It was almost like being back in Olas Altas again, laughing and riding the waves with my friends.

One weekend, Ronnie and I built a skateboard ramp out of wood and metal in his backyard. It was an incredible ramp, two meters tall and six meters across, with a sloping U on both ends. One end had a ladder on the back, so we could climb to the top. We carefully covered the ramp with plastic every time it rained. Emily's mother smiled as she looked out the window, watching me and Ronnie practicing our moves. She liked keeping Ronnie close to home. She had no idea I was a heroin user who was selling drugs on the side.

Ronnie was a good kid. I wanted to teach him how to surf, but I didn't want him to turn out like me. When he came with me and Emily to Redondo, I didn't smoke weed, and Emily and I didn't make out in the back seat.

• • •

In early summer, I knew I wanted to leave Maya. I built a shack under a bridge to the 405 freeway. I fashioned it to look like Donato's shack on Stone Island. Surrounded by bushes, our shack was close to the elementary school park. No one could see us. Even if a few cars spotted us from the freeway, they couldn't stop. If police were looking for us, they couldn't find us. There were no girls allowed.

The shack, about three blocks from Randy's Donuts, was our hangout. Our clubhouse. Our hideout. The place where we could rest and kick back. When I finished dealing drugs about three in the afternoon, I bought donuts and apple fritters to take to the shack. I couldn't wait to be with the guys. I lied and told them I was still working for Daylight Freight Company, just coming off my morning shift.

My surfboard was still at Maya's house, but I slept in the shack and kept some clothes in Emily's closet. Emily made sure they were clean. Her Mom told me I could stay at their house, but I liked the shack better. My friends and I were peaceful and happy. We were also stoned.

"Sometimes this feels like we're in a movie."

"Maybe we are? Did you ever think of that?"

We'd laugh and reach for something else to eat, or drink, or smoke. We loved our hiding place, furnished only with sleeping bags. We had weapons—knives and baseball bats—in case there was a rumble, but it was a mellow place except for noise from the traffic overhead. Occasionally people came looking for us, street people who didn't like us, but they couldn't find us. We'd look at each other and smile as we heard them swearing and thrashing through the bushes, until they finally gave up and went home.

Everyone at Shakey's knew I was smoking weed and drinking beer, but they thought I was otherwise clean. Mondo, Emily's boyfriend from high school, was my good friend. A guy who was into skateboarding, smoking weed and hanging out with us at the shack, he often wondered how I made my money.

"How come I never see you with your uniform on when you come here after work?'

"I keep it in the truck. The company washes it for me."

I was always interested in Emily, but I didn't have anything to do with her until she broke up with Mondo. Even after they broke up, Emily and I never kissed in front of him. He had been her boyfriend and I respected that. I didn't break up with Maya, even after Emily and I became a couple. Emily and I went everywhere together. But she still didn't know my secrets.

• • •

Milo, a skinny, desperate guy that nobody liked, was from Cacalotan, the same town as my father. Four years older than me, he grew up in Mazatlán and now lived in Inglewood with his brother. I didn't like that he told people he was Puerto Rican, not Mexican. I had to kick his ass twice because of that and because he was mostly just a stupid drunk.

Once in a while, I did some roofing work for Milo's brother Felix. I liked his brother. He was an honest, fair boss. Felix was part of our group who hung out at Shakey's after work, and sometimes Milo came along.

The night of my twenty-sixth birthday was a whole night of disturbance. I switched cars with my friend, Raphael, a low-rider guy who was six years older than me. He took my sky blue 1970 Carmen Ghia, and I borrowed his 1960 black and gray Chevy Malibu. His car wasn't beautiful, but it was big and could hold a lot of people. I needed a big car to pick up a bunch of people. I wanted a big celebration.

The party was at Emily's house. We got the party started and then swung by Shakey's to pick up more people. Milo was at Shakey's, drunk and stupid as usual.

"Happy birthday, Neto. Can you give me a ride home?"

"Get in, but be careful. This isn't my car. I don't want you to throw up or pee in the car."

"Don't worry."

We pulled up in front of Milos's house. As he climbed out of the backseat, he said, "I have something to show you." Milo pulled a gun out of his waistband and aimed it right at me and Emily.

"What the hell are you doing, *cabron*?" I kicked the gun out of his hand.

Next thing I knew, Milo was chasing me with a shovel from his front porch, yelling that he was going to kill me.

"Put that down, *pinche barracho*, before I take it away and smash it over your head."

Meanwhile, Emily bent down, picked up the gun from the ground, and pointed it at Milo.

"Drop the shovel before I blow your head off," Emily yelled. She took charge in a way I had never seen before.

I kicked Milo's ass again, and Emily and I went back to the party. We took the gun with us. Milo chased us down for weeks, demanding the gun.

"I'm not giving it back to you. You're too stupid. You'll hurt someone."

I was proud of Emily. But this was not the kind of life I wanted for her or for us. I was leading a double life, sleeping with Maya and Emily at the same time and lying to both of them. I was doing drugs with Maya and then drinking beer with Emily and her friends at Shakey's Pizza. I was using quaaludes to be a super-stud. I was injecting heroin to relax and be laid back after skateboarding with Ronnie and his friends. Even I didn't know who Neto really was.

I was scared of getting caught. I was afraid that Emily wouldn't want to be with me if she knew what I was doing. I was trapped in my own double life. I didn't know how to get out of it. Emily loved me and I loved her, but my actions were bound to keep us apart. I knew my lies would catch up with me. I was a drug dealer and a heavy drug user. Emily was a free spirit. I needed to let her go.

24
Men's Central Jail

Los Angeles, California
1985

I was sitting with two girls, outside my sister's apartment, when I saw three men walking toward me with serious, determined faces. Two detectives in suits, with hands on their hips. Half a block from me was Chango, a gringo from the neighborhood, who knew I was dealing.

"Hey, Monkey Face, what are you doing here on Glasgow Avenue?"

Chango lifted his chin and nodded. I stared him down. My eyes narrowed while I focused on what I needed to do.

Shit. They are coming for me. Stay calm. They are still a block away. Get up slowly. Don't pay attention to them. Don't look like you are hiding anything. Toss your drugs into the parking lot.

I walked to the corner with two bags of heroin. I tried to slide them out of my pocket. I knew if could just get rid of them, I would be okay. I couldn't be charged with possession if I could throw them more than ten meters away.

I heaved my stash over the crumbling garden wall behind the apartments. Over the wall, past the bushes, into a parking lot. One bag sailed across, landing more than thirty meters away into the public lot for big container trucks. The other one didn't clear. It was trapped by the bushes. I clenched my hands as I gritted my teeth. *How could this be happening to me?* I took a deep breath through my nose, to stop the pain in my chest.

I tried to keep my hands steady, but my heart was thumping. My throat was too dry to swallow.

The men in suits ran toward me. Chango stayed where he was. I didn't move. I needed more than luck to get away this time.

"Turn around," one detective said as he patted me down. He searched me but didn't find anything. The other man ran toward the wall, hoping to find the bag that didn't clear. When he found it in the dirt, under a low bush next to the wall, he looked at his friend and laughed.

"Come with us," the detective said.

"That wasn't for me," I told both men, as they continued to search behind the apartments and the parking lot for the second bag.

"Don't tell us you were just holding it for someone. We know who you are."

Chango turned and walked away. "*Chingado,*" I yelled after him. "I'm coming after you."

The detectives smiled. "We've been looking for you for a long time." Their steady voices were quiet. "This game is over, and we won. You are going to jail."

People looked out their windows. My friends ran inside to tell my sister. Cars continued to cruise up and down the street. Mothers walked to the bus stop, on their way to work or to the grocery store. Children held hands as they walked to school. I kept my head up and tried to smile.

I knew there was no way out for me. I didn't have any other income. I couldn't make bail, and I wasn't going to ask anyone for help. *Maybe this will be a three-month vacation for me,* I thought.

I was silent as the detectives walked me to their car. There was nothing to talk about. They didn't need to handcuff me. I knew where I was going.

These guys are just doing their job. If I cooperate maybe they won't check me for needle tracks.

I was arrested for possession of a narcotic to sell, but I escaped being charged for using. The following Monday morning, I appeared before the county judge.

"Mr. Flores, you are hereby sentenced to two years in the federal penitentiary for possession of one ounce of heroin. Because this is your first offense, I am going to suspend that sentence and send you to Men's Central Jail for eighteen months, instead. If you sign up to be a Mayo, you can be out in half that time."

I am going to spend nine months locked up. A summer of no surfing in Redondo. No hot summer nights with Emily and her family. No more pizza and beer at Shakey's. No more . . .

"Thank you, sir."

• • •

Men's Central Jail was a huge facility, housing four thousand people. It was considered one of the worst jails in America, full of Bloods and Crips picked up for dealing crack cocaine and killing each other. I was considered low risk because I was a young, first-time offender and I hadn't killed anybody.

"Flores, welcome to your new home. Stay out of trouble. Don't talk to nobody." The guard unlocked the gate.

The jail was worse than I imagined. It wasn't safe. I knew I could be jumped any time, just because someone didn't like the way I looked. For ten days, I closed my eyes only for a few minutes. I couldn't sleep. I used my long bushy hair to hide my face.

I looked around at lines of bunk beds in a big square. Two lines, forty bunks long, facing each other. Four sections facing north, south, east, and west. There was no one I trusted.

I spent hours talking to myself. *We are all just cattle here, waiting to be classified before going to the next section of the jail.*

Three hundred twenty men, mostly Black, some Mexican, and a few white, were shouting and cursing. Threatening and fighting. I knew I needed to be silent and not part of the background noise. My head hurt from coming off heroin. *Why do these fools need to keep yelling? Why can't they just keep quiet? This is hell. I can't let myself sleep here. Nothing is safe.*

Even at night, after lights were out, men yelled all night long for drugs so they wouldn't be sick. For their families. For public defenders who would never hear them.

Most of the men knew they were going to be sent to the maximum penitentiary in Folsom. They had nothing to lose. I had everything.

"How do I get out of classified? I'm afraid I'm going to get killed in here." I asked the guard. "I want to be transferred to the Mayos."

"You need to go back to court and talk to the judge."

"I'm ready to do that. I don't need to wait for a lawyer. I'm not going to get one. I know I'm guilty. I can talk to the judge myself."

"Okay, I'll tell the clerk. Just stay out of trouble."

• • •

Mayos spent all their time underground, living in the tunnels under the jail, working in the kitchen, prepping food for the four thousand men upstairs. Or sweating in the steamy heat of the laundry. We were like rats and cockroaches, silent and busy as we hurried from place to place.

I have no idea why we were called Mayos, but I was happy to be one. I wanted to work and spend as much time outside my cell as possible. I would have worked all day long if they'd let me.

"Hey, Flores, if you're going to be here, you need to get a job."

"Okay. What do you want me to do?"

"Can you cook?"

"Yes, sir. I'm a good cook. I've been cooking for my family all my life."

"Where are you from?"

"I'm from the hills outside of Hacienda del Tamarindo, Mexico."

There was no way I was going to let the guards know I was from Mazatlán. The city already had a reputation for wild parties and drug use. I wanted the guards to think I was just a stupid kid from the country. Maybe a farmer. Maybe working on the roads, doing construction.

"Here, show me how you cook pancakes."

"Yes, sir." I poured pancake batter on the hot griddle, ten pancakes at a time. When it was time to flip them, I grinned and flipped them so fast I looked like a magician.

"That's good, Flores. What else can you do?"

"I can make French toast. I can make tacos and grilled cheese sandwiches. I can make anything you want me to make."

Guards escorted hungry men out of their cells, in single-file lines, to eat the food that I cooked. I made thousands of pancakes every day. Plus eggs, sausages, and toast. There was a constant, silent parade of men—one line coming in and one line going out of the cafeteria. Inmates were there to eat and we were there to cook. That was all. We signaled for what we needed—more pancakes, more French toast, more sausages. I tried to keep my eyes locked on my stove and not look up unless I heard someone sneeze or cough or clear his throat.

When we got back to our cells, we talked through the bars and in the bathrooms.

"Hey, Flores. Why does the food all taste like crap?"

"Don't you know? It's the saltpeter they put in the food, so we don't get hard-ons."

"Hey, White Face. Can I trade you some of your salt and pepper? I'll give you an extra banana tomorrow when you come through my line."

"Sure. Just make sure it's a good one. I hate them black, mushy bananas."

"Who has some Mexican chili powder to trade for an apple tomorrow?"

"I have some my sister brought me, but I don't want any apples. I'll trade mine for a cigarette."

"What's the matter with the coffee? It tastes like piss."

"It is piss, *pendajo*. Did you see the color?"

Mayos worked hard. We cooked and cleaned up after three hundred people every twenty minutes. My crew served fifteen hundred people every meal. There were two other crews, serving just as many inmates. Breakfast at five. Lunch at eleven. Dinner at five. The rest of the time we sat in our cell. My skin turned as white as my jumpsuit. My hair was long. It took a long time to dry after I took a shower.

"Hey, Flores. Don't you want a haircut?"

"No. Of course not. I'm a surfer. This is what my hair looks like. I don't want to look like one of these gangsters with bald heads."

Three or four nights a week, we were allowed to go up on the roof for an hour of fresh air. For six months, I never saw the sun. I didn't see a sunrise or a sunset. Up on the roof, I could breathe fresh air and look at the moon, but the sun wouldn't come around again until it was time for me to go to work. I tried to remember what blue sky looked like.

We had privileges because we were all Mayos together up on the roof. We could smoke and talk if we wanted to. We knew who was getting out soon and would take messages to people we cared about.

It was a time of peaceful solitude for me. I was quiet. I tried not to think of Chango, the rat who put me in jail, but I knew I needed to find him when I got out. I didn't want to talk about my future. Instead, I transported myself to the cold, foamy California coast. Surfing. Diving under the water and coming up for air. I rode the waves, breathed in the salty air, and swam with the fish in the ocean. I smiled at dolphins and turtles, swimming by. They smiled back.

I looked up at the sky and saw the constellations, just as they were when I traveled across the ocean with Captain Pimienta. Great Bear and Little Bear. Cassiopeia and the Swan. The Archer and the Snake. I sat down on the cement and thought of all I was missing, working underground. The people I loved most knew where I was, but I told them not to visit. I wondered if they were thinking of me.

I made up poems in my head. *I need to be strong. I need to be a better person. I need to find someone to love. I need to find someone to love me.*

As I listened to the other Mayos talk, I prayed. *Dear God, I only want to surf again and stop my bad ways. I want to have a better education and stop using drugs. I want to go to school and find a real job. I want to help everyone I meet. I only want to surf again.*

Sitting together on benches and on the cement, men would start to sing songs we grew up with. The Black guys would sing hymns that I didn't know. My songs, love songs from Sinaloa, were the songs my father sang as he walked home after work. I was happy to be outside, in the dark, with only the lights from the heavens and our cigarettes, so no one could see that thinking about my father made my eyes water.

• • •

I shared a cell with a light-skinned, mixed-race guy we called White Face. Two years older than me, he was a Crip, part of the White Fence gang. He was a huge guy, with a lot of tattoos and a bushy Afro. We each had our own bed against the wall, with a toilet in the middle of our cold cell in the basement. White Face and I worked out a system.

"Hey, White Face. Turn around, will you? I need to use the toilet."

"Can't you do that while I'm in the shower?"

"No. Sorry. I need to do it now."

White Face and I were careful to shower and soap ourselves every day so we wouldn't have to smell ourselves and each other. We were able to talk, but I preferred to be quiet. To sit on my bed, to read or write in my notebook. I was confined in jail and yet I was free. Free from drama. Free from women. Free from drugs and alcohol.

"Hey, Flores, you okay with having White Face in your cell?" I was outside, up on the roof, talking with a guard.

"Sure. We're comfortable with each other. Why?"

"Well, one time we tasered him. He was making a lot of noisy threats and we needed to quiet him down.

He staggered but he never fell. He can be a mean son of a bitch."

"No, we're okay."

I talked to White Face even less after that. We were both in Central Jail for drug dealing. We were pretty much on the same level, but I wanted to make sure we'd get along.

• • •

When I was put in Men's Central Jail, I was fighting with Maya and seeing Emily on the side. I thought maybe I still loved Maya, but I knew I loved Emily more.

How could I let this happen to me? I asked myself the same question, without an answer, every day. I didn't want anyone to see me like this, especially Emily and her family. Just thinking of them made me feel ashamed.

I was used to blaming others when something bad happened. But who could I blame this time? People thought of me as a laughing guy. Carefree and willing to try anything. A charmer with women. A guy who liked to tell jokes and funny stories. Now I was just another pancake flipper living in the basement of the Men's Jail. A long-haired guy with no money and no friends. A surfer in a place where I couldn't see or smell the ocean. I couldn't even see the sun. I was lost in an endless line of silent men, waiting for someone to call my name, for someone to set me free.

I earned extra time off my sentence because I was a good worker. I came out of prison after six months instead of nine, and I wanted to do better. I was determined to stop dealing drugs and to spend my time at the ocean. But first I had to see Maya, to see if she still loved me. And then I had to settle up with Chango.

I didn't tell Maya I was getting out. My car was in a friend's garage. My skateboard, my surfboard, and some clothes were at Maya's. I wanted to surprise her, and I whistled as I walked up to her door. I was eager to hold her and kiss her. To see her smile, to know that she was happy that I was back.

I waited until Maya's girls were in school. I parked my car under a tree and walked up the sidewalk. I gave Maya a loud whistle, my signal that I was home, just as a guy we called Mechanic was coming out the door, buttoning himself up. I knew he'd had his way with her.

"You're an asshole," I said to Mechanic.

"Hey, it's a free country."

I didn't make a fuss. I met Maya at the front door.

"It's over," I said.

"I know. I'm sorry."

I wanted to go to Redondo, to put my board in the ocean, to laugh and have fun again. To be a better person. But now I had two people to see, two separate scores to settle. I fantasized about a clean, carefree life as a surfer, but I had my Mexican pride to defend. I had to prove I was a man. It was worth the risk.

I found my gun, a double-barreled shotgun, where I'd left it with my friend, Honduras, in case I needed protection. I loaded the gun and went to see Chango.

"Where does Chango live? Do you know?" I asked Honduras.

"It's on Century Boulevard. A green house, past Seneca."

I parked the car under a big leafy Amapa tree, lit a cigarette, and turned on the radio. The warm LA afternoon was beginning to turn to night. Thunderclouds formed behind me as Chango opened his front door and saw my car. I knew it was him. He turned away and headed back inside. I could see a shine of sweat running down the back of his shirt.

Chango knew I would come for him sooner or later. Everyone in the neighborhood knew I had to get even with him for putting me in jail. I called his name. When he turned around, I looked him in the eye and aimed my gun right at his face.

Chango spun around just as my gun went off. Gunshots sprayed toward the door of his house and stopped when it hit the metal protection screen.

Maldita sea! I missed him. I missed the son of a bitch.

My aim was off. Some people suggested that maybe I really didn't want to kill him. They are wrong. I thought about Chango every day I was in jail. I wanted him dead. I needed to kill him to even the score.

I never saw Chango again. Nobody did. I kept

waiting in front of his house, but he never showed up again.

Maybe someone else shot him before I had the chance? Maybe the cops took him someplace for protection? Maybe my father's words made me lose my aim?

So many times my father warned me, "*M'hijo,* never kill another man. You get blood on your hands that never washes off."

I wanted to obey my father's words, but I still had to get even with Mechanic. Maya and I didn't talk while I was in jail, but part of me still loved her. Mechanic should have known that because he was my friend. Mexicans have rules between friends, and one of them is that we don't approach each other's girlfriends. If they break the rule, they have to pay the price.

I hated Mechanic. I needed to teach him a lesson. I was furious. I couldn't stop the words playing over and over in my head. *Nobody fucks me over and gets away with it. I am the one who is used to getting away with things. Nobody does this to me.*

I drove up to Mechanic's shop and walked inside, my fists clenched inside my pockets.

"Hey, Neto. I'm sorry."

Before he could say another word, I swung my fist into his face. I knocked him to the ground and kicked him. I kept pounding him, blow after blow, while Mechanic covered his face with his hands

"Neto, stop! You're going to kill him!"

Who was talking to me? A man? A woman? I knew it wasn't Maya. It was just me and Mechanic inside the shop. I turned around and walked out the door.

My next stop was Mechanic's house. He wouldn't be home for a while. He wasn't going to come out of the shop until he knew I was gone from the neighborhood. His wife answered the door. Her lips were painted bright red. Her eyes were dark and laughing.

"Come in, Neto. I wondered if you would come to see me."

"Yes, I thought I would stop by and say hello."

"I heard you caught my husband coming out of Maya's house."

"Who told you?"

"Neighbors. Friends. It doesn't matter. You know, my husband wanted to have something to do with Maya even before you went to jail."

"I thought so. I should have kicked his ass when I was still living here."

"I know a better way to get even."

Mechanic's wife took me into her bedroom. We shared a joint and had sex right there. When I heard him come home, I got up and passed him as he came through the door.

"There. Now we're even."

• • •

A week went by before I worked up the courage to see Emily again. She knew I had been in Men's Central Jail. The whole neighborhood knew why, and I was embarrassed. I needed to apologize to Emily and her family for what I had done.

As I got out of the car, Emily ran out the door and down the sidewalk to meet me. She hugged me and stroked my hair. Her mother and Ronnie were right behind her.

"Neto! You came back." She kissed me long and hard, right in front of everyone.

"Can we go for a walk?"

Emily and I walked around the neighborhood, holding hands. She asked me about my time in jail, but I didn't want to talk about it. I wanted to apologize. To forget. To start over.

"Is Ronnie still the best skater in the neighborhood?"

"Absolutely he's the best! He still practices every day on the ramp you built in our backyard."

We talked about our friends. We slowed down as we neared her house. I wanted to hold her. To be together again. I wanted to be the person Emily used to think I was, but I had just gotten out of jail. I didn't know if I could be that person right away.

"I have something special for you when we get back home."

"What is it?"

"It's from all of us. You'll be surprised."

When we got back to Emily's house, a lot of our friends were there. Ronnie called them and told them I was back. They were laughing and happy to see me. Emily handed me an envelope.

"What's this?" I asked.

"Open it." Inside was $450 in cash. "It's for you. We want you to have it so you can start over."

I had a lump in my throat. I didn't know what to say. No one had even been that generous to me before. I knew I didn't deserve it.

"Thank you. This is a lot more than I need."

"But we want you to have it."

"I have a better idea. Let's all go to Shakey's for pizza!"

Emily and I continued to be friends, but I decided to stay away from her. She was young and innocent. I needed to be alone, to surf and think, to become a better person.

25

Paloma

I first met Paloma in 1984, before I was sent to Men's Central Jail. I was still living with Maya, seeing Emily on the side, dealing drugs, and sleeping in the shack under the highway. Mamí knew I was headed down the wrong path. She wanted me to meet someone who went to church, worked hard, and loved her children.

Mamí worked for a couple in Echo Park, José and Lupe. She took care of their boys, cleaned their house, and did their laundry, while Paloma rented a small *casita* directly behind their house. I noticed her coming and going through the gate between the two houses when I visited my mother. On the side of the house was a patio with a clothesline that they shared. I saw the two women talking and smiling as they hung wet clothes to dry in the wind. *Who is this pretty woman who doesn't even look at me?*

"I want you to meet Paloma. She's a good woman.

With three kids." Mamí looked up from warming tortillas on the *comal*.

"Does she have a husband?"

She does, but he's in Folsom for a long time."

"A long time? Why?"

"He killed three people. But he only was charged
for murdering one of them."

Everyone in Echo Park knew Paloma's husband.
He was a big, ugly Cuban guy. One of the convicts
that Fidel Castro sent to the US in the seventies.

Originally from Cuernavaca, Paloma's face was a
mask sculpted out of copper-colored clay, smooth
without any marks. Her onyx black eyes shined like
the morning star. She was short and a little *gordita*
from having three kids right in a row. Her straight
black hair, cut off at her shoulders, curved and
bounced when she shook her head from side to side.

I would have been happy to get to know
Mamí's neighbor, but Paloma didn't give me any
encouragement.

One morning, I stood with my mother in the
shade of their avocado tree, smoking a cigarette and
talking before she started her chores. I was laughing
and joking when my mother put her hands on my
arms and looked in my eyes without blinking.

"Neto, this is serious. I need you to help Paloma.
She's been gone a month."

"Sure. What can I do?"

"She's is Tijuana. She needs to get back to the US."

"What's she doing in Tijuana?"

"She went to visit her mother in Mexico for maybe the last time. Now she needs to get back, but she doesn't have papers. I know you help people get across."

"Where is she in Tijuana?"

"I told her to call me tonight. You can talk to her when she calls. Or give me a message and I'll tell her what to do."

"Let me talk to her."

Was Maya suspicious of where I was going? Who I was going to meet? Maybe. But Maya was used to me coming and going, sometimes for days at a time. I didn't tell her why I needed to go away for a few days and she didn't ask.

"Neto, it's me. Paloma."

"Hi. Where are you?"

"I'm at the Hotel Emperador on Calle Coahuila, downtown Tijuana."

"Stay there. I'll meet you tomorrow at four o'clock."

Paloma's voice was soft and sweet, not like Maya's clucking voice of an angry duck. I wanted to get to Tijuana right away. I wanted to take care of Paloma and bring her back with me to Echo Park.

"Listen to me. I'm coming to get you. No worries. Everything's going to be fine."

Paloma was waiting in her room when I arrived. She smiled, but her eyes were wet and squeezed shut so I wouldn't see her cry. Her chin quivered when she started to talk.

"Neto. Thank you for coming."

"Of course." My heart was warm, beating steady under my shirt. "I've done this before. I brought what we need."

"Can we go tonight?"

"I don't think so. The river is high and running fast. It is better to wait until tomorrow. I can stay at my cousin's house and come back in the morning."

Paloma's sweet face collapsed. She blinked back tears. "Neto, I'm afraid to stay here another night by myself. I don't think I'm safe."

"Don't worry. I can stay here with you. We won't sleep together. I'll be on the floor, next to the bathroom. We'll leave tomorrow night, I promise. My friend Ricky will be waiting for us on the other side."

The next night the water was still running fast when we got to the riverbank. But there was no moon, only clouds high in the dark sky, and no other people going across when we got to the water's edge.

"Don't be afraid. I'm going to get you across safe, but you need to do what I say. You are going to get wet, so take off your clothes and put them in this plastic bag."

"Even my panties?"

"No, you can leave your panties on."

I looked around, alert to the sound of Mexican thieves or worse, *la migra*. "Wait here," I whispered. "I'll be right back."

The current was fighting me, and the river was cold as I stepped into the water. I held our plastic bags over my head. Everything we needed for the other side of the river was in those bags. Dry clothes and shoes. Towels and two water bottles.

I hurried back. "Okay, are you ready?"

"Neto, I can't swim."

"No, baby. You aren't going to swim. I'm going to walk you across the water. You need to climb on my shoulders. Wrap your legs around me. I'm going to hold onto the front of your knees. Grab my hair and don't let go. If the current gets too strong, I'm going to swim us across."

"Neto, I'm not sure."

"We can't talk any more. Here, get up on my shoulders. Don't worry. My head is going to be underwater some of the time. Stay still and let me carry you across. Once we are on the other side, you are safe. No one is going to jump us on the California side."

We crossed the river and ran straight to the rocks. We were both breathing hard. I looked around, searching for police.

"Here are your clothes. Dry yourself off real good. Throw your wet panties in this bag," I put on dry shorts and a T-shirt before going back to the river to fill our bottles with water.

Paloma shivered as I poured water on her legs and feet. "Use this towel to make sure you don't have any wet sand on your legs or between your toes. If agents stop us, they will be looking for sand. They can't find any or they'll know we just came from the river."

Coyote Ricky met us there on the rocks in less than an hour. He brought two tickets to the train, just like I told him. The crossing was over. We were safe and on our way back to Echo Park. We climbed into the backseat of his big Buick Century and silently closed the doors. Paloma fell asleep, her head on my shoulder. I smiled and leaned toward her. I couldn't get the smell of her panties or the feel of her skin out of my mind.

• • •

A year later, I came out of Men's Central Jail and was embarrassed to see Paloma again. We didn't talk about where I had been or that I had broken up with Maya. Everybody knew about those things, so we didn't need to talk about them.

"I missed seeing you, Neto, while you were away."

"I missed seeing you, too."

"I wish you could find a job near here. I feel safe when you are around."

"I'd like that, too."

I saw more of Paloma after that. We often talked when I went to Echo Park to see my mother. Sometimes I would find both of them hanging wash on the same clothesline, exchanging recipes and gossip about the neighborhood.

Mamí was another person who wanted me to get a job. "*M'hijo*, you need to work and make some money. An honest job, so I don't have to worry about you."

"I know. I don't want to go back to my old ways. I need to stay away from Inglewood. I'd like to find something here in Echo Park."

My mother nodded her head. "Echo Park would be good for you. You already know Paloma and the people in the neighborhood. It's a place for second chances."

"Let me know if you hear anything."

"I know José is looking for a guard for his impound shop. The last guard died while you were in jail. Maybe he would give you the job."

The impound shop was a big garage, right next to Paloma's yard. Tow trucks dropped cars there until the owners paid a fine to get them back. The garage took up a whole block and held at least a hundred cars in three separate spaces.

I went to see José. "Hello. I heard you needed a guard."

"Do you have any experience?"

"A couple years ago I worked in Sandy, Oregon, guarding a welding shop and strawberry fields."

"Do you think you can guard these cars?"

"I'm sure I can. I've been working since I was twelve."

"I know that. Your mother told me that you are a hard worker and you like being around cars. She won't forgive me if I don't give you a try."

It was a good job. I took in the cars and kept track of where they were parked. I made friends with the tow-truck drivers and the police. The best part of the job was that it included a place to stay—a tall wooden boat that was impounded and left outside the shop.

The boat became my home for the next fifteen months. It had been a sailboat, but the mast was taken off and stored inside the garage. Still on the trailer, the boat sat straight up on six wheels. It must have been someone's pleasure boat, but it was mine now. It was pretty inside, with wooden walls and two bedrooms, a little kitchen, and a bathroom. There were two entrances, both with removable steps. I went in and out the back side, so no one knew if I was there or not.

I was on duty all day, every day. I carried a beeper because the boat had no phone. At night, if a tow-truck driver needed to talk to me, he called Paloma's house. I got a dog to help me guard the shop, a black-and-gray mutt named Rusty. The dog and I played catch with an old, slobbery tennis ball or a chewed-up Frisbee during the day when we weren't busy.

I talked to Paloma every day. I admired her and the way she was a good mother. I respected that she put her children to sleep before she answered my knock on her door.

"Neto, shhh. *Los niños* have just gone to sleep."

"Can I come in?"

"Here. Let me fix you something to eat."

"No, it's okay. I already ate my mother's cooking at José's."

"We have some rice and beans left from dinner. I'm going to warm them up for you."

Paloma's rice and beans were the best I've ever tasted. Onions, tomatoes, and chiles floating in spicy bean gravy, thick with white rice the way the Cubans ate it. We talked for a while until I finished eating.

"Neto, I'm sorry. I can't talk any more. I have a lot of sewing to finish before tomorrow."

Paloma sewed in a factory while her children were in school. Often, she brought clothes home to finish at night, sewing until midnight to make extra money. She was working to get her green card and worked hard for very little money.

"Here, let me help you. What are you sewing tonight?"

"Sweatpants."

"We can do them together. If we finish early, we can go lie down."

"Okay, Neto. But you need to leave before morning. I don't want anyone to see you walking out of my house."

Even though Paloma's husband was in prison, in her mind she was still married to him.

"Do you still love him?" I whispered in bed at night.

"I don't think I've ever really loved him."

"What happened?" I wanted to know about her life. I wanted someone to love me the way I loved Paloma right them.

"I had just come here from Mexico when I met him. Raul was older and very powerful. He wanted to have me, and I let him."

"Why didn't you leave him? Go somewhere else?"

"Neto, I told you. He was very powerful. And I was pregnant."

"Did you get married?"

"Yes. In the church. And the next year I was pregnant again. And the year after that. If he hadn't gone to jail, I'd probably have six kids by now."

"Did you know he was a criminal?"

"I knew he was stealing. He used to wake me up when he came home at two, drunk and shouting. Showing me jewels and whatever he had stolen. I didn't know about him killing anyone, though."

"But why do you worry about him now? People say he's in prison for at least twenty-five years. He's not coming out."

"Neto, you don't understand. Some of his gang friends live in this neighborhood. If they tell him about you, he can still hurt me or the children. He could have us killed. He's a very jealous man."

In the beginning, I didn't even make a pass at Paloma. I liked her a lot, but I was galavanting all over town and she was married. As months went by, we started sleeping together, and once in a while we had sex, but we always used protection and there were no commitments. Paloma was content with our friendship. She didn't want more. Just like she never wanted the fancy expensive things her husband brought home. She only wanted a good life for her children.

Paloma's hands, with long graceful fingers, were strong. Made for work, for creating beauty, for taking care of her family. Like the peaceful dove she was named for, she was a woman with a golden heart, full of nothing but love and kindness.

Paloma went to the Catholic church on Sundays, and she prayed every night before we went to bed. She prayed for her children and the rest of her family. She prayed that her boss would like her work and approve her for a green card. She prayed for José, Lupe, and my mother. And she prayed for me. I looked away when I saw Paloma on her knees, praying in her soft, quiet voice to the Virgin.

"Please, señora, help Neto stop smoking weed. He tells me that he isn't, but I can smell it on his clothes. Help him, too, to stay out of trouble and be the good person I know he is meant to be." If Paloma knew I was using cocaine with some of the women I met, she would have been praying twice as hard for my soul.

Paloma even prayed for her husband. I prayed for him, too. I prayed that someone would slit his throat in jail and Paloma would be mine. I never told her about those prayers, or she would have told me to pray for forgiveness.

Twice I took Paloma and her two younger children to Folsom Prison to visit Raul. He called the house a lot, always demanding money and visits.

"Neto, I think I have to go see him. Can you drive us?'

"Sure. Why do you want to go?"

"I feel like it's my duty."

"I know. I understand."

We left Paloma's oldest daughter at home. Palomita was old enough to see what was happening between me and Paloma. If Raul had asked questions, she might have told the truth.

The trip took eight hours each way. Folsom is twenty miles outside of Lake Tahoe. With the kids talking and laughing in the backseat, we drove for three hours and then stopped. Then we drove for three more hours and stopped again. I waited outside while Paloma and the children got in line to go inside. I hated the guy, but I didn't want my sweet little dove to worry. I only wanted to make her happy. To put smiles on her pretty face.

Paloma knew what I was doing when I wasn't with her. She didn't like my meandering ways, but she never accused me of anything or made a fuss. When I was with her, we held each other and kissed. I caressed her arms and rubbed the knots out of her back.

"I'm sorry, honey, for the all the things I do."

"It's okay, Neto. I know. You are a man. Not a priest."

Paloma had a lot of family in the neighborhood.

Her house reminded both of us of growing up in Mexico. Cousins laughing and playing together every weekend. Running through the house, in and out of the back door, asking for food and something to drink. Paloma's nieces stopped by all day long with questions.

"Paloma, can you fix my dress on your sewing machine?"

"Paloma, how do you make your carnitas taste so good? Can you show me how?"

"Paloma, you better keep an eye on Palomita. She's getting older and you know how the men in this neighborhood are going to start looking at her."

"Paloma, I heard that Neto was at Renee's house last night. Did you know that? Why do you still let him in here?"

Even though we were really careful, a lot of the neighbors, mostly her cousins and nieces, gossiped about me. We never hugged or kissed in front of the children, but the neighbors knew what was happening and wouldn't stop talking. I was a rooster, and the women didn't like me strutting around the neighborhood.

I liked Paloma's children, especially her son Marcos. He was six years old when I moved to Echo Park. He had the same beautiful copper skin and black eyes as his mother. He was a thin, quick, athletic boy. We played soccer together, in the street. I taught him to throw a ball. To ride a skateboard and then a bicycle.

227

We talked a lot about cars and trucks. Marcos loved my Chevy Nova. When he was in sixth grade, I came back to Echo Park and taught him to drive.

Marcos was happy, smart little boy who loved school. When I started walking him to school every morning, I felt like a stepfather to him. I wanted to be the father he didn't have. We talked on the way to school, and I tutored him after school in subjects like arithmetic and science. I was proud of him, and I think that, in a way, he was proud of me, too.

• • •

In 1986, a year after I started working at the impound lot, Paloma and her family complained to me about a disgusting *Chilango* from Mexico City, who was drunk all the time in his car.

The *pendejo* lived in his car and parked it on our block, often in front of José and Lupe's house. He stunk so bad I covered my nose when I talked to him. He never took a shower or shaved his *feo* face. The smell of cheap tequila oozed out of his skin, and his feet smelled like fungus in his flip-flops. I hated him because he polluted the neighborhood and peed on my avocado tree.

One day the old fool saw me talking to Vivian, a new girl in the neighborhood. He knew that I wanted to kiss her, even though I was sleeping with Paloma.

"I know you want to kiss her. Go ahead. You're

going to lose. She won't kiss you back. She'll slap you instead."

"*Escuchame, hijo de puta,* I'll make you a bet. If I kiss her and she kisses me back, you gotta leave. Leave this neighborhood and never come back."

"That's a bet. I'm staying right here."

The whole neighborhood heard about our contest. They pulled back their curtains and watched out their windows, waiting for Vivian to walk down the street. They stood in their yards, behind jacaranda trees and hibiscus bushes.

Vivian stopped in front of my shop. "Hola, Neto. *Como estás?*"

Just like that, I leaned into her and kissed her on the lips. She kissed me back. Fireworks exploded in my brain. The neighbors clapped their hands and cheered.

"That's it, you old fool. Now you gotta leave."

"No. I think I'll stay right here."

"Oh, no you won't."

I started pushing his car. The neighbors came running. We pushed his car, with him inside, all the way down the street. The lady who lived next door to my shop was so happy she kissed me and sold me a used Renault for seventy-five dollars.

As the summer moved into fall, Paloma saw that Vivian and I were falling in love. We spent hours talking in front of the impound shop. We held hands and shared food from the taco shop down the street.

Paloma let me know that she approved. She wanted me to settle down, stop cruising around the neighborhood, and maybe start a family.

"Neto, I am happy for you. You have always been my dear friend. When you are happy, I am happy."

• • •

Now I'm an old man back in Mexico, my country filled with beautiful people, topical flowers, and colorful birds. With poverty, corruption, and crime. Every morning, I sit on the patio, drink my coffee, and smoke my first cigarette of the day. I listen for the cry of the beautiful, round doves, quietly singing their sad *coo-coo-cu-roo*. A sound so sad it should make my heart hurt, but instead, it makes me smile. I remember Paloma and Marcos, who filled my life many years ago with love and hope and peace.

Back in California, I believe my hardworking, sweet Paloma, her hair now salted with gray like mine, is still making the best rice and beans in Echo Park, caring for her grandchildren, and praying for all of us—that we will find our mate. That we will be faithful and stay out of trouble. That we will be the people we were meant to be.

26

Vivian

Los Angeles, California
1986–1987

It was a time of extreme passion, tremendous joy, and overwhelming deceit. When I first met Vivian, she told me she was seventeen. She wasn't. She was a child. When I met Vivian, I told her that I was Italian. I wasn't. I was from Mexico.

I was working as a guard at a tow-truck impound lot, but I told Vivian I was the son of the owner. She told me she finished high school. I told her I did, too.

None of this was true. We both wanted to seem important and sexy and grown up. We were playing a dangerous game. One that was bound to end badly.

Nothing about our beginning was the truth except that we were in love. That much I know was true. From the first time I saw Vivian, I couldn't stop thinking about her. My heart pounded, wanting her to be mine. I should have realized that my only true love would be the ocean.

I was twenty-six years old, one year out of jail, and ready to be married. Or so I thought. Marriage for me was like waiting for a taxi. When the right one pulled up, going in my direction, I would jump in and go for a ride. In 1986, I was sleeping with a lot of girls, but none of them were going in my direction.

"Neto, when are you going to stop chasing women? I hear talk every time I go to the store," my mother scolded me. "You said you were going to be married by the time you were twenty-five."

"Don't worry, Mamí. I'll be married soon." I smiled and kissed her cheek. "I'm ready but the right person hasn't shown up yet." Not until that day when Vivian kissed me back in front of the auto impound shop.

I watched Vivian walk toward me on a day hot enough to burn the soles of your feet on the sidewalks of Echo Park. She noticed me standing in front of the impound garage. She was a tall, pretty girl with long, powerful legs. Her straight brown hair brushed her bare arms as she looked straight at me and smiled.

Caramba! *Who is this girl? Why haven't I seen her before?* She had no *chichis*, but that was okay. I was attracted to her sultry brown eyes, her full pink lips, and her clear voice, with no accent in either English or Spanish. I had never felt that excited about kissing a girl before. My whole body was on fire.

• • •

Vivian spent summers in Echo Park, living with her grandparents in a neighborhood mostly of people from Cuba, Mexico, and the Philippines. Drug sellers worked the streets in front of nuns who ran Queen of Angels Hospital. Children walked to school, holding hands, saying goodbye to parents boarding buses to work in downtown stores and taco stands. Neighborhood restaurants were owned by brown-skinned men frying onions and chiles, cooking pots of beans and rice. That was Echo Park in 1986.

I lived in my abandoned boat, parked in front of the impound shop, and I went to see Paloma at night. Before I knew Vivian, I met her grandparents, Diego and Velma Ruiz. I often saw them walking slowly up the street, holding hands, talking and smiling with their heads bent toward each other.

Diego walked with a limp. Sometimes, when he was out walking alone, he stopped to rest on the steps in front of my boat. I sat next to him, each of us smoking a cigarette, talking like two men in no hurry to go anywhere.

Diego was a quiet, gentle Filipino man, with short, thick, straight black hair. He reminded me of my Mexican uncles, back in La Hacienda.

"Sir," I asked as he took another drag on his cigarette. "Does your leg hurt when you walk?"

"Sometimes. If I walk very far, my leg hurts more than usual."

"Were you born like that? With a limp, I mean."

"Oh, no. This is what the Japanese did to me in the war. They threw me in a mass grave, but I wasn't dead yet when Velma found me."

"How did she know where to look?"

"Someone saw the Japanese dumping a lot of people into a pit. They were covering the bodies with lime. Most people were dead, but I wasn't. I was still alive."

"How did you get out?"

"I held my breath and crawled to the edge of the grave. Velma found me there and dragged me all the way home."

Diego and I were friends for a long time after that. I invited him to go to the Santa Anita and Hollywood Park racetracks. Sometimes I gave him an extra twenty dollars to place bets for both of us. Even though Velma was a great cook, sometimes we'd sneak off to McDonalds and Burger King for a cup of coffee and a hamburger with fries.

• • •

After our first exciting kiss, it was a summer of love for me and Vivian. A time of sweetness even though the lies continued. Vivian and I were silly together. One time I bought a new pair of Bermuda shorts for fifteen dollars. Vivian said that as soon as she saw those red-and-orange shorts, she knew we would always be together.

We flirted and kissed. We laughed and told stories. We got to know each other, but we didn't have sex. I still had other girlfriends, but of course I didn't tell Vivian. I hung on to my secrets. She hung on to hers.

As the summer wore on, Vivian told me that she was not happy. "I don't want to go back to Arizona. I hate my mother and stepfather always telling me what to do. I want to stay here with you."

"I want to be with you, too, but I think that first you need to go back to say goodbye."

Vivian was looking for someone to take care of her, and I wanted to be that person. I was looking for someone to marry. Someone to love.

In August, Vivian went back to Arizona. Before she left, I called her mother.

"Hello, I'm Ernesto. I'm a friend of your daughter. I like her a lot. I have a steady job, and I would like her to be my girlfriend."

"Yes, Ernesto, Vivian and her grandparents have told me about you. I think she already is your girlfriend."

"Well, yes, that's true. I want you to know I will take good care of her. I've kissed her but that's all."

"I hope that's all, Ernesto."

"I have a question. I'm not sure how old she is. She said she was seventeen, is that right?"

"Yes, that's right."

"I'm going to miss her. Is it okay if I call her on the phone?"

"Yes, Neto, but Vivian needs to stay in school. She is a good student, even if she is a rebellious daughter. The most important thing to me is that she graduates high school."

"Thank you, ma'am. I will make sure that happens." That was when I knew that Vivian didn't finished high school. It was okay. I didn't either.

Vivian called me at Paloma's house from pay phones outside her mother's house. She said she didn't want to call long distance from her mother's phone. She didn't want her mother to know how often we talked. Our calls were short, often interrupted by the clink of more quarters being dropped into the pay phone on her end. I was excited just hearing her voice. I thought about her every day. At night, I went back to roaming Echo Park, like the neighborhood black cat looking in garbage cans for something to eat.

In December, Vivian came back to Echo Park for Christmas vacation. We went to the movies and held hands. We shared a bag of popcorn and a box of Milk Duds. I remember the smell of her hair. The touch of her skin. I rubbed her arm in long, slow strokes, and she squeezed my hand. I remember every detail of that first real date, except the name of the movie, the actors, the setting, or what it was about.

After Christmas, my life was full of changes. I left my home in the boat and my job at José's impound garage. I went to work part time as a guard for an auto repair shop, owned by Esteban, a man from Columbia. Besides guarding, I was doing some body work, mostly painting and repairing scratches. I was happy there and was making good money, $300 a week, working from ten to four. The most I'd made from José was $200 a week for guarding all night.

In the spring of 1987, I moved to a beautiful apartment in downtown LA. I'd never lived in such a beautiful place before. It had an elevator and carpet everywhere, even in the hallways. The rent was $450 a month. I was happy to pay it. I wanted to have a beautiful place for Vivian and me to live.

My landlady, a gorgeous Columbian girl, was married to a big-time cocaine dealer from Mexico City. I got to know them and forgot my determination to live clean. The coke dealer and I partied a lot—with plenty of pretty girls and drugs. I made runs with him. Sometimes he sent me out alone. He only sold coke, nothing harder, and I never bought any from him. I only distributed what he had to sell. I knew I would have to leave my wild ways behind when Vivian showed up. In the meantime, I was making good money and having fun.

The other five guys working in the auto shop were all from Mexico. We loved our jobs, working on very fancy cars—Cadillacs, BMWs, Porsches, and Mercedes, mainly. The cars were brand new, with only a little damage from being in accidents. We wore white jumpsuits to protect us and the cars. The boss gave us lunch every day, usually tacos and chicken, but we could have whatever we wanted. We had a gym to work out in. Nobody acted suspicious, and we never thought there was anything illegal going on. We were clean. But the shop wasn't.

Near the end of school year, I talked to Vivian's mother again. "I would like to come and pick up Vivian at the end of the school year and drive her to California. Is that okay?"

"Yeah. You can take her with you. She's been nothing but trouble here. Maybe you and her grandparents can talk some sense into her."

"Thank you, ma'am. I'll try."

Vivian and I talked on the phone. The plan was for me to pick her up in Prescott and drive back to Los Angeles. I gave my word that I would be there for her.

"Pick me up at my friend's house," Vivian told me over the phone. "I'm living there now."

"Is everything all right?"

"Yeah, but I couldn't live at home anymore. I'm all packed and ready to see you."

This was the first time I knew that there was more than just a little trouble at home. Vivian didn't tell me until I picked her up that she ran away a month before I got there. She also didn't tell me that she dropped out of high school. She knew I would be upset if she told me, so she didn't. And, as she told me later, "I didn't need your permission."

I borrowed a car from my friend Memo at the

auto shop and left LA early in the morning. I wanted to avoid the heat from the desert. I drove straight through, stopping for gas once, but I didn't need anything to eat. My stomach was dancing with butterflies. There was nothing to see except yucca and a few dead animals on the road. I turned the radio up high and stepped on the gas.

I found Vivian at her friend's house, sitting on the side of the swimming pool, dangling her feet in the water. We both opened our arms wide as she ran barefoot in the grass to meet me. I got a hard-on as soon as I touched her. I was embarrassed and didn't want anyone to notice, but they probably noticed anyway.

I stroked Vivian's hair, still wet from the pool, and rubbed her warm back. We kissed, but I was shy about kissing her in front of other people. We held hands as she introduced me to her friends.

Vivian wanted to leave right away, to get away from Prescott and her family. Her packed suitcase was waiting by the front door. I wasn't tired at all, only a little hungry.

We jumped in the car and sped away to Phoenix, where we rented a room, found a place to eat, and stayed for two nights. We had sex the first night. It felt so good to be together that we couldn't wait anymore. I don't know if Vivian was a virgin or not. It was better not to know.

We stopped in Tucson on our way home because my brother Pablo was living there with his family. I wanted Vivian to meet my brother and his family. We were very shy. We held hands, but we wouldn't kiss in front of Pablo's kids. We also wouldn't kiss outside the car. But inside was okay.

We stayed with Pablo's family in Tucson for three days. I called Vivian's mother to tell her that her daughter was with me and we were on our way back to LA.

"Okay, Ernesto. Thanks for letting me know. Good luck. Drive carefully."

It was time to return the car to Memo. We checked in with Vivian's grandparents and went to live in my fancy apartment. The next day I went back to work at the auto body shop.

About a month later, after Vivian and I were settled in our new apartment, one of the workers, Manolo, borrowed a car to run an errand. The car broke down along the highway to San Bernardino. The sheriff came and searched the car. Inside, they found $5 million in jewels, stolen in New York and ready to be transported to Columbia.

Manolo called me in a whisper, almost out of breath. "Neto, you and the other guys need to get out of the shop and go home right away. Take all of your shit with you."

"Why? What's going on?"

"You know the car I was driving? It was full of jewels. I was arrested. They let me go, but I had to tell them where the shop is. They are coming to search. You guys need to disappear."

By the time the police came, we were gone. Only Esteban, the owner, was still there when the police found all the expensive cars, stashed with drugs, money, and stolen goods.

It was time for me to get a new job and find us a new place to live. In the meantime, Vivian moved in with her grandparents and I lived with my sister Alicia while I looked for a new job.

27

Lunch Truck Leo

I needed to find a new job. Any job. Maybe two jobs. I was trying hard not to go back to selling on the street. It had been two years since I left Men's Jail, and I was mostly clean, except for smoking weed when I could. Vivian hated drugs. She knew my history. She wanted me to leave those ways behind me.

My mother was no longer working in Echo Park. Now she lived on the same street where my sister Alicia worked. Every morning Lunch Truck Leo delivered coffee and breakfast to Alicia's jobsite. I stopped at the truck whenever I was in the neighborhood visiting my mother.

Leo, the owner, was short and dark, with a scruffy beard and a mustache right under his nose. Originally from Chihuahua, he wasn't quite thirty years old. He and I joked as I stood outside his window ordering coffee and *pan dulce* or a breakfast burrito. He liked my ways, and I had fun with him, too.

"Hey, Neto. I need to ask you something," said Leo, stroking his bearded chin. "I see you around here almost every morning. Do you need a job?"

"Yeah. I need to find something to do." I clasped my hand around my warm cup, wondering what Leo was saying. I scuffed my feet on the pavement, waiting for him to talk.

"Well, I need someone to drive this truck for me. Are you interested?"

Sure, I was interested. I needed a job. Leo told me he needed a driver because he was caught driving the truck while he was drunk. I didn't have a driver's license, but he didn't ask about that.

Leo offered me $120 a day, plus a place to live, in exchange for driving his truck around the city. He and his wife owned three apartments on top of a parking garage. Vivian and I lived in the guest apartment for free. We were happy to be living together again. Our place was one bedroom with no kitchen, separated from Leo by a sliding glass door. With my first paycheck, I bought a motorcycle that I parked in the garage.

Vivian and I locked the glass door in the morning, and went to work on the food truck together. She didn't feel safe in the apartment after Leo made a pass at her. I told him to leave her alone, but I still didn't trust him.

Every day, except weekends, we left the house at 4:15 a.m. and rode my motorcycle to pick up the lunch truck. Leo's Grill was a full-service truck with an oven and a grill. We had ice for sodas and a big coffee pot. We had a cook on board to make burritos. When the cook didn't show up, Vivian was the cook.

I liked driving the big lunch truck, but I began to see that Leo was really a creepy guy. He asked me pick up drugs for him late at night. He would pound on my door and demand that I get him drugs and women. I knew people in the middle of the route, drug dealers and hookers, who gave me good deals that I passed on to him.

Sometimes Leo would pay for two or three women at a time. When I brought them home, he wanted to share them with me.

"Neto, be a man. Show this girl what you have," he demanded. His words were sloppy from booze. He stumbled in his bedroom slippers as he staggered toward me.

A few times I slipped and had sex with a couple of his girls just for fun. I knew that it wasn't right. I was embarrassed and ashamed when I went home and crawled in bed next to Vivian.

I covered a lot of territory in Leo's truck. There were twenty-five stops in all, and some of the stops were twice a day. When the customers arrived, I took cash and kept tickets for the people who bought on credit. It was hard to keep track of the money and drive the truck through traffic at the same time, but I did it.

The meat packing plant was my first stop at six in the morning. As soon as the guys heard my horn, they streamed out of the building to buy burritos on credit. I always gave them free coffee.

At night I would go back to the meat packing place to collect money. The workers were big, strong guys with huge muscles. The looked like NFL players. They were allowed to buy meat at half price from the plant. Sometimes they would show Vivian one of their steaks and ask her to cook it for them.

The meat packers often paid their bill in meat. Steaks, filet mignon, layers of New York strips.

"Neto, here's five steaks for you. The rest are for Leo."

Vivian would cook one steak for me. Alicia would buy the rest to take home and cook for her boyfriend.

One day Leo's girlfriend called me, desperate, from the school where she was a teacher. She was hysterical, sobbing and gasping on the phone. I liked Carolyn as a person, but I never looked at her for anything else.

"Neto, you need to help me. I'm stuck here at school."

"What's the matter?"

"This damn car isn't working. I can't get it started."

By this time, I had a little white VW convertible I bought for running errands when I didn't want to use my motorcycle. I jumped in the car and found Carolyn standing by the flagpole outside her school. Fixing her little AMC Hornet was easy for me. I was able to get it started right there in the parking lot.

"Thank you, Neto. I knew you could fix it. I don't know what I would have done if I couldn't find you."

"No problem."

"Here, let me pay you something."

"No. You don't owe me anything." I was happy to help.

Later, Carolyn told Leo that I had something to do with her. She said I made a pass at her and tried to kiss her.

Leo barged into our apartment, swinging a shotgun in my direction.

Vivian came out of the bathroom. "Neto, what's going on?"

"What the hell are you doing?" I shouted as Leo pointed the gun at me.

"I'm going to kill you. That's what I'm doing. You leave my girlfriend alone."

I pounded my fist against the wall. I wanted to pound it into his fat ugly face.

"You only have one shot, *pendejo*. If you miss me, I'll take the gun away from you and blow you away for real."

Leo backed away. I risked everything. I didn't own a gun, and I knew Leo had three of them. But Leo knew I was serious.

"I quit. Find someone else to drive your *pinche* truck. Vivian and I are leaving and taking the Hornet with us. You want to get killed, come after the car."

Vivian saw the whole thing happen. After it was

over and Leo left our apartment, Vivian turned to me. Her face was pale. Her lips and chin trembled. She couldn't keep her hands still as she reached out to touch my arm.

"Neto, what are we going to do?"

"We're getting out of here."

"But where? We can't stay here. We don't have a job or a place to live."

"We're going to take Carolyn's Hornet and go to Paso Robles."

Leo never said anything. Leo and Carolyn both knew I was innocent. I didn't go after other people's girlfriends. It was my code. I broke it once, when I came out of jail, but I never did again.

28
Joshua

Los Angeles
1988–1989

My cousins were picking grapes in Paso Robles in the Salinas River Valley of California. Vivian and I drove up just as the early grapes were ready to pick. We parked the Hornet in front of the owner's cabin and went inside to ask for work. We were young and eager, and the owner felt like he already knew us. Rodriguez men from Sinaloa had worked in the grape fields for generations. We were hired right away.

We stayed in Paso Robles through the grape harvest, from August to October. It was hot and dry when we got to the fields, and the heat never left. On weekends, Vivian and I drove to the coast, twenty minutes away, where I was able to surf the frigid water of the Pacific Ocean. We found a small apartment to rent and went out to the fields every day, picking grapes from early morning until sunset. Away from Leo and the hustle of the city, Vivian and I started to feel like teenagers again. Working hard, side by side, brought us closer than ever. At night, sitting outside under clear California skies, we talked about where life might take us next.

• • •

We left Paso Robles after the final harvest in October 1988 and moved back to Los Angeles. Vivian lived with her grandparents for a couple of weeks, and I lived in my car. I found a security job, working twelve hours a night, two nights a week—guarding apartments, condos, and occasionally parking lots. I went to see a man I knew from Echo Park, and he hired me to work as a maintenance man for a section of bungalows that he owned. My life was good. I had a steady income and a girlfriend I loved. I was clean and wasn't being chased by anybody. Vivian was content living with her grandparents, and I was happy living in the AMC Hornet that I took away from Leo.

By December 1988, it had been more than two years since I first fell in love with Vivian, more than a year since we started living together. We had been trying to get pregnant for a while. We never used protection, but Vivian still didn't get pregnant.

"Do you think something's wrong?" I asked her. "Maybe you can't get pregnant."

"I don't know. I think it just isn't the right time."

"*Chula*, it's okay."

"No, it's not, Neto. I know you're disappointed."

"No, I mean it. Maybe next month."

We tried to get away on weekends, little trips to the beach, sometimes stopping in small towns along the way.

"I got some extra time off. Let's go to Las Vegas for the weekend."

"What will we do there?"

"I don't know. Maybe gamble a little. We can drive to Reno first. It's a pretty drive."

Driving to Las Vegas through the Sierra Nevada mountains on a two-lane highway was a new route for me. I hadn't planned on the drastic weather change, and the Hornet didn't have snow tires. I hung on tight to the steering wheel as the road turned to ice and snow going over the pass before dropping into Reno.

We got to Reno, and Vivian didn't look good. I thought maybe she was sick or nervous from riding through the mountains.

"I feel funny, Neto. Can we stop at the Planned Parenthood clinic? I see the sign for it across the street."

"Are you sick?"

"I don't know what's the matter. I just don't feel good."

Vivian came out of the clinic smiling. "Neto, I'm pregnant. Three months pregnant. We're going to have a baby in June."

We grabbed each other, laughing and both talking at the same time. I kissed her and told her I loved her. That I was proud of her. That I couldn't believe it. We were going to have a baby.

We left Reno and I knew what I wanted to do in Las Vegas. I didn't ask Vivian to marry me. I made the decision to marry her, and I knew she would say yes.

"I'm going to take you someplace you've never been before. I know you will like it."

Vivian didn't answer me. She had fallen asleep. She woke up as we were coming into Las Vegas.

We went to see the justice of the peace in the courthouse. Later, although we were already married, Vivian and I decided to get married in a chapel, just for fun. We grabbed a couple of witnesses. I don't remember if I bought Vivian a ring or if we wore special clothes. It was a quick, silly ceremony, but I was able to tell people that now, finally, I was a married man.

I couldn't wait to tell everyone back in LA that we were expecting a baby—Vivian's grandparents, my sister, my friends, Paloma and Marcos, my mother and her former employers, José and Lupe. I told clerks in the stores and people I met on the street. I couldn't wait for our baby to be born.

I was the happiest person around. The feeling I had was pure joy. Time stopped for me. There is no way to explain how happy I was. I had never felt like this before. My happiness was so huge I couldn't count it in numbers. I went to the sky and jumped for the stars. For the first time, I felt like I made my mother proud.

From that day on, with Vivian pregnant and knowing she was my wife, I became a changed man. I wanted to satisfy her. Vivian was my wife, and I wanted to take care of her and our baby. I thought about her all day and dreamed about her at night. I had too much energy, even for me. We moved into an apartment on Rosamond Street in West LA, one block away from Diego and Velma. I was always working, either at home or at one of my two jobs. Vivian got a job at Burger King in downtown LA, working five hours a day until Joshua was born.

On weekends, when neither of us were working, we spent all our time together. We were both happier than we expected to be, and we started to be nicer to each other. We spoke softly and laughed a lot. Little by little, I stopped getting action on the side. I made a decision to stop using marijuana. I had been a sneaky dog, but when Vivian got pregnant, I decided to quit all my bad ways. Loving Vivian made it easy.

Vivian was healthy and happy. She was healthier than me. Healthier than a horse. She blew up like a balloon. She was so big I thought we were going to have three babies.

In early June, the doctors said our baby could come any day. Vivian wasn't sleeping, and I didn't sleep much either. The day Joshua was born, Vivian made herself busy around the apartment. She cleaned the kitchen and straightened up the living room, carrying dishes to the sink to be washed and put away.

She wiped down the stove and the countertop. I took her to her grandparents' house before I left for work.

Velma called me at my job, to tell me that Vivian needed to go to the hospital. I was there in five minutes.

"Are you okay?"

"My water just broke."

"Here, don't bend over. Let me clean it up. Don't slip."

We drove to Children's Hospital, where Joshua was born. He was a precious, little baby boy. I couldn't wait to hold him in my arms.

I was twenty-nine years old, scared about being a father and silly with joy at the same time. Soon after Joshua was born, the nurse brought him to Vivian's room. He opened his eyes as I said his name. I gazed into his brown eyes and stroked his head. I smoothed his straight black hair with my hand and said a blessing over him.

I stayed with Vivian for an hour, and then I went back to work. The next day I took Vivian home and took the day off from work. From the minute he entered this world, I loved Joshua with all my heart.

Vivian stayed home to take care of our baby for three months, and Velma and Diego came every day to help take care of the baby. I smiled driving home, thinking about seeing Vivian and Joshua again. It was an easy, mellow five-minute drive for me. For the first time in my life, I worried. *Did Joshua have a good day? Did Vivian? Did the baby cry too much? How would I know if something was the matter?*

I talked to myself above the hum of traffic and used that time to think. I made a pact with God. I prayed to the Virgin of Guadalupe and the rest of the saints. *Please, all you saints, help me to be a good father. A good husband. Help me to grow up and leave my selfish ways behind.*

I kissed Vivian as I walked through the door and said goodbye to Velma, who hugged me before grabbing her purse and heading out the door.

"Where is Joshua? Can I hold him? Does he need his diaper changed?"

Vivian laughed as I picked up our baby. "Of course, you can hold him. At least until he's hungry again."

Joshua was a perfect baby. He hardly ever cried. Drinking Vivian's milk, he smiled at me with the nipple in his mouth, milk dribbling down his chin. When he was finished, I took him in my arms, put him over my shoulder, and patted him until he burped and fell asleep.

There is a big, deep breath that babies take just as they fall asleep. It is the sweetest music on earth.

"You can put him in his crib now. Let's have something to eat."

But I didn't want to put Joshua down. I combed his beautiful, thick black hair with my fingers. I rubbed his cheek. I breathed along with his breath, keeping time, breath by breath, until he was fast asleep.

Only when I knew Joshua was fed, in a dry diaper and asleep, did I pay attention to Vivian. I was a foolish man. I wanted so much to be a good father, I didn't think enough about being a good husband. I stopped using marijuana and seeing women on the side because I knew Vivian didn't like it. I should have done more.

Vivian was kind. I knew she loved me. She was proud of me and proud of our son. She wanted only the best for us. I didn't realize what it was like for her, a young mother at home with a baby to care for all day. At night we talked about Joshua. I told her funny stories about my work. I didn't ask her if she worried, like I did, or if she missed her life in Prescott—being in school, laughing with friends.

29

Mr. Washington

When I was still with Paloma, I started walking her son to school. Marcos and I held hands as we walked along the sidewalk—me dressed in sweatpants and a bright Hawaiian shirt and Marcos in long pants and a freshly ironed, long-sleeve shirt.

Echo Park before school reminded me of early mornings in Mexico. Women outside sweeping the sidewalk or splashing water from a bucket onto their plants. Trees and flowers giving off their sweet smells along the boulevards. A few restaurants ready to open but others still shuttered for the night. Doors slamming shut as men and women hurried to work, not all that eager to get there. Tiny birds sang to us as we talked about the day ahead.

Mr. Washington, the school principal, greeted us every morning.

"Good morning, Marcos. How are you this morning?"

"I'm good, Mr. Washington."

Marcos, the son of my girlfriend, Paloma, was six. He was the same age I was when I was a student in the military school in Tepic.

"And how are you, Ernesto?"

"I'm great, sir. You can call me Neto. How about you?"

"I'm fine. But you should probably keep calling me Mr. Washington."

Mr. Washington was an athlete. He jogged for thirty minutes every day before school. A man in his mid-fifties, he had a headful of white hair with a little bald place in front. His white mustache wiggled on his lip when he talked. He wore a suit with a nice shirt and matching tie to school every day, in contrast to the drug users and homeless people who walked past his school as he greeted his students.

"Are you ready for school today, Marcos?"

"Yes, sir."

"Did Neto help you with your homework last night?'

"Yes, sir. He helped me with my arithmetic sheets."

"Did he help you with your reading?" I watched Mr. Washington smile. Marcos kicked the dirt with his shoe. He watched it rise in tiny dust storms and settle back down on the sidewalk.

"No, sir. Neto talks good English, but he can't help me much with reading and writing stories. My mother helps me when she gets home at night."

"No wonder you are such a good student. Someday

ERNESTO FLORES

you are going to grow up to be somebody, Marcos. I know it. And Neto knows it, too. Now go ahead and walk inside. Your teacher is waiting for you."

Paloma left early to go to work at the sewing factory. "Don't worry, sweetheart. I can walk over from the shop and stay with Marcos and the girls until it's time for school to start."

"Thank you, Neto. Marcos needs to be around someone like you. He feels safe with you." She smiled and gave me a quick kiss. "I do, too."

I walked Marcos to his classroom and came back outside to talk to Mr. Washington for a few more minutes. Mr. Washington was a happy guy. I liked talking to him before going back to work.

"Where are you from, Neto?"

"I'm from Mazatlán. But I've been living mostly in the US for ten years."

"How do you know Marcos?"

"I live next door to Paloma and her kids. She's my sometimes girlfriend."

"Sometimes?"

"Well, when I'm not with someone else, I'm with Paloma."

"Is that okay with her?"

"I think so, sir. I never asked her."

"You take good care of Marcos. I've noticed that. I like that about you."

Mr. Washington and I talked like this every day before school. He was the principal, but he was also

258

the crossing guard. One day I volunteered to take his place.

"I'm happy to be the crossing guard, Mr. Washington, if you need me to be here."

"No, Neto. I love this part of my day. I want to make sure that all of my students get here safe and on time."

"It's the best part of my day, too," I agreed.

Little by little, Mr. Washington and I got to know each other. "How did you end up working at the impound lot, Neto? Do you like it there?"

"I got that job after I came out of jail. It's a good job for me. I want to leave my bad ways behind me. I like working, and Paloma is a good woman. Being with her helps me stay clean."

"Do you want to do this for a long time? What about your future?"

"What I really want is to have a family. I told my mother I would get married when I was twenty-five. I'm already twenty-six, but I haven't met the right person yet."

"I think you will be a good father, Neto. Make sure you find the right person."

• • •

I stopped by to talk to Mr. Washington sometimes, even after I left Paloma and Echo Park and moved to LA with Vivian. I wanted Mr. Washington to get to know my new girlfriend. He frowned when I first introduced her to him. He looked at me with wide-open eyes and raised his eyebrows.

"This is Vivian, Mr. Washington. She's my new girlfriend."

"I'm glad to meet you, Vivian." They shook hands. "Neto is a good man. I hope you take good care of him."

Even after I didn't need to walk Marcos to school anymore, Mr. Washington put a smile on my face every time I thought about him. I remembered him again two years later, in 1988, when we were back from picking grapes and I needed a job.

"Hi, Neto. Where've you been?"

"I've been mostly in LA. I drove a lunch truck for a while, but that didn't work out."

"Really? Why not?"

"My boss's girlfriend told a big lie about me, so I had to leave."

"Are you still with your girlfriend?"

"Yes, sir. We just came back from Paso Robles."

"So, what brings you to Echo Park? Are you here just to say hi?"

"No, I'm here because I need a job. I'm working two days a week for a security company, but I need to do more."

"What are you thinking you'd like to do."

"Is there anything for me here at the school? I can do maintenance. I can help on the playground. I like being around the kids. Is there anything I qualify for?"

"No, Neto. I'm afraid you need to be legal to work in the school. The school board will never hire you."

"Oh, I'm sorry. I don't think I will ever be legal."

"But wait a minute. I might have a job for you where I live. I'm looking for a maintenance man to work on my property."

"That would be great. I think I'd like that."

"Come back here after school. I'll take you to see my place. When we are off school grounds, you don't have to call me Mr. Washington. You can call me by my name: Darnell."

Darnell had plenty of property—a big house and eleven bungalows. And money from his renters to pay me.

"It looks like you need a lot of work here."

"I need you, that's for sure. But first, I need to make sure you can do the job. How about this? You will be on probation for two weeks. You'll work for free. Then, if I decide to hire you, I'll pay you ten dollars an hour plus social security."

"I can do that."

"One problem, Neto. I'm worried about your girl-friend. She looks very young to me. Are you sure about how old she is? To be honest, I think you should dump her."

"I can't dump her, sir. I married her. She's going to have my baby."

Darnell kept me busy. I did gardening, and I re-paired decks and sprinkler systems. Everything needed painting all the time. The place was a jungle land, weeds and bushes growing everywhere. I fixed up the landscaping in three months. I chopped and shaped the bushes. Some of them I cut down. I cleaned up the rubble and trash that people threw everywhere.

"This looks great," Darnell told me one afternoon. He was home from school and had changed out of his formal principal clothes into a pair of shorts and a T-shirt with a collar. He had a magazine in his hand.

"I'm thinking about putting a fishpond in here," he said. "Do you think we can do it?"

"Of course. How big of a pond do you want?"

Darnell showed me a picture in the magazine he was carrying. My eyes popped open. I had never built a pond that big or that beautiful before.

"I'm thinking about ten feet by twenty feet. With a waterfall and plants, and maybe some fish."

I started digging the hole. I dug it by hand to fit the plastic tub that Darnell brought home from somewhere. He ordered rocks for the waterfall and a pump to keep the water clean and moving. Together, we stacked the rocks so that water would cascade down in a splash as it hit the bottom.

"What about all the leaves that fall in the water?" Darnell asked me. "Do you want to scoop them out every day? Or is there something else we can do?"

I certainly didn't want to spend all my time scooping wet leaves. We put a net over the pond and a canopy at one end, with chairs under it for people to sit in. It was a masterpiece. Whenever I think of working for Darnell, I remember that fishpond with the waterfall.

• • •

My baby, Joshua, was born in June. I couldn't wait to bring him to work with me. Even the bikers congratulated me and told me what a good-looking boy he was.

"Neto, why don't you take Joshua to the bungalows while I visit my grandparents," Vivian offered.

"Don't you want to come along?"

"I'm not comfortable being around Darnell and the renters. You go. Pick me up on the way home."

The bungalows were rented to some of Darnell's friends, a bunch of bikers—mostly reckless, stupid, lard-ass people who threw their trash all over my beautiful landscaping. Finally, I put up big trash barrels with lights over them. I never said much to the bikers. I just did my job and took out the barrels of trash every night before I went home to Vivian and Joshua.

Until I started working for him, Darnell looked just like anybody else to me, but when he introduced me to Ruco, I knew right away that Ruco was gay. Then I realized that Darnell might be gay, too.

Ruco was a geezer. A crabby, old, white guy. He looked a lot older than Darrell. I think he was about seventy years old. He was tall and skinny, with lots of wild gray hair. I was uneasy around him. Growing up, I didn't know any homosexual people and I didn't like the idea of them. If we thought someone was queer, we usually caused trouble for him. I was afraid of getting AIDS, so I avoided touching Ruco and the other gay people who came for parties on the property.

• • •

Soon we had two babies in diapers. My second son, Nico, was born in September 1990, three months after Joshua turned one. I kept working for Darnell and Ruco. I painted and repaired the bungalows. I kept trimming trees and mowing the lawn. I remodeled rooms in their big house.

Darnell and Ruco liked to throw big parties, and they had a lot of friends. I got over being afraid of gay people when they invited me to stay and drink with them before I went home. Darnell's home became a shelter for me. I loved my boys, but being married wasn't as much fun anymore. Vivian and I were fussing at each other, and the boys were a lot of work. Sometimes I'd stay at the bungalows for two or three hours after work before finally going home.

Darnell was a good boss. He wanted the job done right. He paid me every day in cash. He gave me raises and extra payments. One time, when I was arrested after a fight with Vivian, he visited me in jail and gave me money in case I was deported.

"Neto, I hate seeing you in jail," he said. "I hope you learned something by sitting in here instead of coming to work for me."

"I did, sir. I hate being here. I know I shouldn't have grabbed Vivian, but I was afraid she was going to stab me again with that damn screwdriver."

"Maybe you shouldn't have made her so mad in the first place?" I felt like I had just been called into the principal's office. "She's young and impulsive. You married a girl with a bad temper. Now you have to love her in spite of it or leave her because of it."

"Is it really that simple?"

"You don't have to make it complicated."

"Then I guess I'll go home and stay with her. I can't stand the thought of not having Joshua and Nico around for me to hold."

• • •

In 1991, Vivian and I took the boys on a plane from LA to Mazatlán, each of us holding a little boy in our arms. By this time, Joshua was two and Nico was one. I was eager for my father and my friends from Olas Altas to meet my new family.

Everyone loved Vivian right away. I was proud to introduce her as my wife. She tried surfing with me.

We went to Stone Island to relax and to the beach so the boys could play in the sand. I wanted them to learn that the Mexican ocean was different from California.

Darnell gave me a month off. It was his idea to have my younger brother, Cachi, work instead of me so I could take a vacation. Cachi was my favorite brother, fun-loving and carefree. He followed me to California the year before. He wanted to leave Mexico and see if he could make a living in the United States. He often visited my mother and sometimes stopped at the bungalows to see me. Darnell liked him right away. I knew Cachi was smoking weed, but we all were. I didn't know that he was also using cocaine.

When I came back, Darnell was furious. "Neto, your brother is a thief."

"Oh, no. What did he do?"

"He told me we needed five thousand dollars' worth of new tools from Sears to do the work around here."

"You didn't give it to him, did you?"

"He's your brother, Neto. Of course, I gave it to him."

"What happened to the tools?"

"What do you think happened? Your brother stole them. I don't know where he is. He doesn't answer his damn phone."

"I'm sorry, Mr. Washington. What can I do to repay you?"

"You can keep working here until you pay off this debt. That's what you can do."

"I will do it. I will make sure you are paid off. Please tell Ruco I'm sorry."

I worked hard to pay them back, paying at least $200 every payday for more than a year until Cachi's debt was paid off. Darnell began to trust me again, but Ruco never stopped growling and hissing at me like an angry donkey.

I knew how to find Cachi. He was living in a house in Santa Monica, with guys he'd met drinking on the beach. I didn't call him to let him know I was on my way to see him. I drove down his street and saw Cachi's truck parked outside. I didn't give him a chance to see me before I banged my fist on the door and walked in. Cachi jumped up from his bed on the couch, where he was watching television turned up loud.

"Cachi, you fool, turn off the TV. I'm going to kick your ass," I shouted.

"I'm sorry, Neto. You probably should. It might make you feel better."

"Nothing is going to make me feel better. You're my brother. I gave you a good job and you destroyed me. Darnell was my friend. Now he doesn't even want to look at me."

"I'm sorry, Neto."

"No, you aren't. What the hell did you do with the money you got? Why did you tell him you needed new tools?"

"I bought the tools and showed them to Darnell. I wanted a new lawn mower and clippers for the yard."

"That doesn't cost five thousand dollars."

"Some of the money I kept."

"So, what happened to the lawn mower and everything else you bought?"

"After I showed them to Darnell, I took them back to Sears and got the money back."

"And then?"

"I used the money to buy cocaine."

• • •

I said goodbye to Darnell and Ruco in 1992. My marriage was in shambles. Vivian wanted to go back to Arizona. We both had been scared by two big earthquakes that shook our neighborhood, but that wasn't the real reason Vivian wanted to move. She wasn't happy living in California. Raising two young boys, she was trapped in an apartment with a husband who loved the ocean more than he loved her. It wasn't the life she had dreamed of. She had hopes for her future. She needed to get away from me.

"I've been talking to my mother on the phone a lot lately. She wants me to come back home so she can help me take care of the boys."

"You know you don't like your mother. Why do you think this is going to work?"

"She sounds better on the phone. I think maybe we can get along now that I'm older."

"Won't it be hard for you to leave your grandparents?" I knew it was going to be hard for me to say goodbye to Darnell, Ruco, and the Bungalow Boys. I would miss Vivian's grandparents, too, and I certainly didn't want to see her mother.

No matter what I argued, Vivian was firm. Neither of us wanted a divorce. I didn't want Vivian to take the boys and go to Arizona without me.

"I want this to be a fresh start," she said. "I think we should try it."

I wanted a fresh start, too, so I agreed. We both meant well, but by that time, it was too late.

· · ·

I stopped by to see Mr. Washington in the mid-1990s. I was back to my old ways. One time, stopping on my way to California, I was carrying $5,000 from selling drugs. I think he could tell from my eyes that I was embarrassed to see him. I was no longer the guy who used to walk Marcos to school. They guy who was proud of his life. The guy who built the fishpond.

30
Nico

In October 1990, four months after Joshua was born, our lease was up on the big house on Rosamond Street and we had to move.

"Where should we go?" Vivian asked.

"Maybe we can go to Carson. From there, it's easy to get to Long Beach and Redondo."

Carson was twenty miles away. Away from Velma and Diego. I knew Vivian wanted to stay close to her grandparents, but we needed to find something cheaper. I liked being married, but I missed being near the beach and my surfing friends.

"What about my grandparents? They will miss being with Joshua every day."

"We can drive up to see them every weekend."

"It's going to take you longer to get home from work. I'm going to need help with the baby."

"I'll come home as soon as I can. Joshua is an easy

baby, and you are a good mother. Call me if you need me and I'll come home right away."

"Okay. But remember, I still need to finish high school. And after high school, if there is a community college, I want start right away."

Moving to Carson made sense to me. I wanted Vivian to finish high school and go to college. I wanted my kids to go to the beach. I wanted to live close to Redondo so I could go surfing and get extra work from Donato on the weekends. We stayed in Carson for a full year.

• • •

Six months after Joshua was born, Vivian was pregnant again. We were excited to have another boy. Again, she was healthy and never sick when she was pregnant. She went back to school and got her high school diploma in time for Nico to be born.

With another boy, my joy was doubled. The day Nico was born, Vivian called Paloma's house. Her daughter, Palomita, answered the phone.

"I need Neto to come home and there's no way to call him. He's working at the bungalows. I'm going to the hospital. Please, find Darnell at school. I want Neto to meet me at the hospital."

Palomita ran all the way to Darnell's school. "It's an emergency," she told the office secretary. "I need to see Mr. Washington right away."

"Mr. Washington is talking to a student, but you can go in."

"Vivian is having the baby," Palomita shouted as soon as she walked into the principal's office. "She needs Neto. The neighbor took her to the hospital in Carson."

Darnell called Ruco and told him I should leave work because Vivian was having our baby. I grinned so hard I thought my cheeks would split open. That made Ruco mad. He was almost always pissed off anyway. He hated to see me so happy.

It was a cool September day in 1990. The hot summer days were going away. There were lots of low gray clouds in the air, and rain sprinkled lightly on the dirt as I ran to my car.

It was a thirty-five-minute drive on the freeway from the bungalows to Children's Hospital in Carson. I jumped in my car, the same AMC Hornet that I drove to Las Vegas two years before. I drove so fast trying to get to Children's Hospital, I burned up the engine. Luckily, I had enough velocity that I was able to cruise to the off-ramp and onto a side street. I left the car on the side of the road, grabbed all my stuff, and walked the last mile along the freeway. The doctors told us that the birth might happen fast this time.

I arrived at the hospital, still carrying all the things from my car. I wanted to be there when Nico was born, but I was too late. Nico was a little smaller than Joshua. He weighed six pounds. Joshua weighed six and a half. By the time he was two, Nico looked just like me. I looked into his mischievous black eyes and saw myself looking back.

I watched my boys as they learned to crawl, then stand up, then take off walking, swaying from side to side like they were drunk. Then one day they jumped up and start to run. They both had strong, sturdy legs. Nico was another sweet, happy boy, and Joshua was a protective big brother. With two babies to love, we were a growing family.

Vivian stayed home and watched our two little boys. She didn't go back to school as we had planned. I worked at Darnell's bungalows, driving back and forth from Inglewood to Carson. Sometimes I got home late. Vivian was a good mother and a good wife. I hope I was a good father. I loved the boys, and I loved Vivian. I wish I had been a better husband.

31

Strangers

California and Arizona
1992–1996

Our lives were going to change. I knew that, and I didn't want to believe it. We were married but we weren't lovers. We weren't even best friends. We were strangers. Our only connection was the two boys, our sons, who lived in our house as if nothing had changed.

Vivian stayed home with Joshua and Nico all day while I worked two jobs to support us. My life was full of interesting people. Her life was full of diapers, dirty dishes, and soap operas. Vivian resented that I came home when I wanted to and that the boys were excited to see me when I walked through the door. I resented how much time she had to stay home and play with them.

I could tell that Vivian was not happy. She started running away from home, just like she did when I first met her. The first time, she took off in the car with the boys and didn't tell me where she was going.

I called her grandparents, and they didn't know where she was either. Later that night, she called me and said she wanted to come home, but I was furious.

"*Maldita sea!* Don't ever do that to me again. It's a disgrace to me. You make me look like a fool."

The second time she ran way, I didn't look for her, and Vivian came back home on her own.

• • •

While I was working for Darnell, I started doing side work for a guy named Larry, some bodywork and painting cars. I didn't tell Vivian how much money I was making. I didn't want her to spend it while I was at work. Instead, I hid the money I made and gave it to my mother, who had bills of her own to pay.

One time Larry let me borrow a car to take another guy, Pelon, home after work. Pelon got his name because he was so bald his head was shiny in the sun. Pelon and I had worked on the car all day, and I wanted to drive it. It was a sweet, classic car, a 1963 Lincoln Continental—white with switch doors. I felt like a king. Like Elvis. I laughed as Pelon and I drove that beautiful car down the highway, windows open, White Snake blaring through the speakers. As I skidded to a stop in our driveway, Vivian came screaming out of the house, her face sweaty and red, holding a long screwdriver over her head like a knife.

"Who is that woman you have in the car?"

"Wait! Stop! That's not a woman. It's my friend, Pelon. Put down that screwdriver and take a look."

I was afraid Vivian was going to scratch the side of that gorgeous car. Instead, she started chasing me through the yard. I ran like the devil was after me. When I stopped suddenly and turned around, Vivian plunged the screwdriver into my stomach.

"*Perra*, what did you do that for?" I grabbed my wife and threw her on the ground.

"Don't kill me," she screamed.

I didn't want to kill her. I didn't even want to hurt her. I wanted her to stop yelling and give me the screwdriver. Blood was slowly oozing through my shirt. I heard sirens coming toward us. Someone must have called the police.

"They're coming for me," I told Vivian. "Call Larry and tell him to pick up the car. There's money under the mat. I just got paid from working on this car. I was going to give it to my mother, but you take it. You are going to need it."

While I was sitting my ass in jail, I had time to think. *How are Joshua and Nico now that I'm not home? What is their mother saying about me? Do they miss me when it is time to take a bath? Does Vivian lay down with them at night, like I did, until they fall asleep?*

The boys were becoming unruly. Velma and Diego came every day to help Vivian take care of them, but they were a lot to handle. They were cute but full of mischief. I wanted to be home.

Vivian called her mother and told her I was in jail. *Did she tell her that she stabbed me? Or did she just tell her I was smoking weed and not coming straight home from Darnell's after work?* That was true. Lots of times I stayed to have a beer with Darnell and Ruco after work. The truth was that I liked being with them more than being at home. If it hadn't been for our little boys, I might not have gone home at all.

I was in jail for two months. I got out just before two major earthquakes hit LA on the morning of June 28, 1992. First the Landers earthquake hit at 5:00 a.m., and then, three and a half hours later, the Big Bear hit. The day was just getting started when we heard the rumble. Dishes fell out of the cupboards and crashed to the floor. The walls began to move toward us. I looked up and saw the ceiling light swaying back and forth.

"Quick. Grab the boys. We've got to get to the sidewalk."

Vivian grabbed Nico from his bed. I hauled Joshua over my shoulder like a fireman would, and we sprinted out the door. Our neighbors, mostly Filipino women, rushed into the street, wearing only their underwear.

The Landers and Big Bear earthquakes scared us as we watched our neighborhood shake and buildings crumble. In the months that followed, Vivian and I both came apart at the thought of another earthquake.

"What happens next time? What if we are trapped in the building and can't get out? Or, even worse, what if we can't get the boys out in time?"

I worried about my boys being safe, growing up in LA. We both felt it was time to leave LA, but where should we go?

"I think we should move to Arizona," Vivian suggested. "It's safer there."

"Okay, but not Prescott. Your mother hates me. I can't live that close to her."

"What about Tucson?" By this time, my brother Cachi was married and had moved to Tucson with his new wife.

"Okay. We can try living there."

Although we both were afraid of another earthquake, I knew Vivian really wanted to live closer to her mother. Joshua and Nico were still little boys, two and three years old. Joshua was potty-trained, but Nico was still in diapers. Even with help from her grandparents, the boys were acting up.

I wanted to help raise the boys, but I had gone back to my bad ways. I was smoking a lot of weed, and the police were following me. I slept with a few women, and Vivian couldn't trust me. We decided that maybe moving to Tucson would help avoid another disaster. But the real disaster was our marriage.

I don't think my boys realized anything was wrong after we moved. I hope not. They played with each other and made friends in day care. They continued to look like normal, happy little boys.

Vivian was not any happier in Tucson, and soon we were fighting more than before. She ran away again. This time she took the boys with her and hid in the shadows. I didn't go looking for her. Instead, I took off and went for a surfing vacation in Mazatlán. Vivian and the boys came home before I did.

I had a good job in Tucson, working at Augustino's restaurant, but I wasn't a good husband and Vivian was miserable. Our marriage was no better than it had been in California. In many ways, it was worse. It's surprising that it lasted as long as it did.

Vivian took the kids and moved back to her mother's home. I drove from Tucson to Prescott every two weeks to spend time with the boys. I no longer loved Vivian, but I always loved my rascal boys.

One day, as I brought the boys back from playing in the park, Vivian came out to the car to meet us.

"Guys, go inside with your grandmother. I need to talk to your father about something."

"What?"

"I've decided to join the army. I've wanted to for a long time. I need to get some training. I've been meeting with a recruiter and this week I signed the papers."

"You did this without talking to me first?"

Vivian laughed. "I really don't need your permission."

"What about the boys? Your mother can't stand me."

"I know. I've decided to let you have them while I am gone. I'll be at Fort Bragg. North Carolina. You can have them until I get back."

I took the boys back to Tucson, and a friend watched them while I was at work. I was working at Augustino's restaurant and was happier than I had been in a long time. Every day with the boys was heaven for me.

I couldn't wait to get home at the end of my shift. I woke them up in the morning and made their favorite breakfast, scrambled eggs and hot dogs. At work, I dreamed up things we could do together on my days off. We splashed in the pool and drove to the desert. We played soccer. We picked up rocks in the parking lot and collected tiny cars. I was excited when I thought of the ultimate activity for them: a trip to Mazatlán to swim in the ocean. We went to Mexico and stayed for two months. I wanted them to remember me and remember Mexico as a place that was fun for boys, three and four years old.

When Vivian came back from Fort Bragg and realized I had taken the boys out of the country without her permission, she lost her mind. I knew our marriage was over, but I was feeling all sweet and tender as I walked my sons up to the wide wooden door of her mother's expensive house. Vivian was waiting for me, hands on her hips. I knew that look. I'd seen it often. Her dark eyes were cold and full of contempt. She stared at me and slowly shook her head back and forth as if I was one of the kids.

I held my boys' hands as we walked up the sidewalk. Her mother was standing in the doorway, directly behind her. I let go of their hands, and my boys ran to stand behind their grandmother, who was blocking the doorway. She pushed the boys behind her and glared at me without saying a word.

"What is the matter with you?" Vivian yelled. She didn't care who heard her. "Why did you think it was okay to take these kids to Mexico? I should have you arrested."

I knew I'd made a mistake. I knew Vivian would never forgive me. But I was still a father to Joshua and Nico.

"When can I come back and see the boys?" I wanted to know.

"I never want you to see you back here again," Vivian growled.

"I don't want to see you either. But I still want to see the kids."

Before I could say anything more, Vivian shouted, "You are nothing to me. Nothing but an illegal Mexican. If you ever come around this house again, I will shoot you."

I took a step back. My lips pinched tight as I shook

my head no. I didn't know what to say. *Can this be true? Is this the same Vivian who ran away from this fancy house to be with me? Will the boys be okay without me? Will I be okay without them?*

"If you come around here again, I'll blow your head off."

Her words beat on my chest like fists. Like she was holding my head underwater. I wanted to reach out to her, to hold my boys one more time. To say I was sorry. But I couldn't breathe. Air squeezed out of my chest. I dropped my head and walked back down the sidewalk.

Inside my truck, blood throbbing in my temples, bile rose in my throat and I thought I was going to choke. I opened the door to get rid of that horrible spit. I looked back to where Vivian was standing. The door was closed, and she was gone. I turned the key, stepped on the gas, and sped away, determined to stop my heart from hurting. I wanted to kill someone. I wanted to die.

That was the last time I ever saw Vivian or my boys again. My life was never the same after I said goodbye to my boys for the very last time. It left a hole in me that could never be filled. Not by drugs. Not by alcohol. Not by having two other children. Nothing could ever take the place of my two little rascal boys.

• • •

A few years ago, I learned that Vivian and the boys believed I was dead. She went looking for me in Los Angeles in 2002. I don't know why she wanted to find me. Somebody who knew me back then said that when I didn't return to LA for five years, they all assumed I was dead. A big part of me was.

32

A Letter to My Sons

I called my boys Rice and Bean. Joshua, with Vivian's long black hair and cinnamon skin, was my Rice and Nico, who looked like me, was my Bean. They were bright lights in my life full of mistakes. Unfortunately, they weren't able to save me from myself.

Dear Joshua and Nico,

I am your father. You don't remember me because the last time you saw me you were still little boys. Joshua, you were four, and Nico, you were only three.

When I dropped you off that day at your mother's house, I didn't know it would be the last time I would see you. I believed I would see you again. Instead, I drove away and abandoned you when you needed me to stay. I missed all the important events in your life. I never called you. I never wrote to you. I didn't even send you a card on your birthday. I was selfish and thoughtless. I hurt you and I am sorry. Sorrier than words can ever say.

After I left the US in 1997 and came back to Mexico, I put your picture on my wall, right by my bed.

Only then did I realize I might never see you again. I didn't know how to call you, and I wasn't allowed to come back to the US to look for you. But I never forgot you. During that same time, you believed I was dead. What a mess I made of my life. What a mess I made of my love for you.

You don't have my last name, but you have my DNA. You are not in my life, but you will always be in my heart. I am proud to be listed as your father on your birth certificates. You were wonderful sons. You made me smile. You gave me nothing but joy. I am sorry I was not the father you deserved to have. I can't ask for forgiveness. Even that would be selfish on my part. If you never want to see me again, I don't blame you. Our separation is all my fault.

Please know that I will always think of you, every day of my life. I have cleaned up my behavior, but that doesn't undo the sins of my past.

I pray that you are safe and that you are better fathers than I was.

I pray that you do not make so many mistakes and that you are not haunted by my same demons.

I pray that someday, in this world or the next, I will see you again.

Amor para siempre, tu padre,
Ernesto Alonso Flores Rodriguez

33

The Accident

Tucson, Arizona
1993

The day Vivian told me I couldn't see my boys again was the beginning of four years of bad decisions on my part. I blasted the radio as I peeled away from the curb and drove away. I gripped the steering wheel to keep my hands from shaking. I knew Vivian had a gun, and I believed she was crazy enough to use it. My only thought was to get home as fast as I could, to get raging drunk, and to pretend this wasn't happening.

The next day was a bright yellow August Sunday in Tucson. The sun was hot on my face as I rested my elbow on the open window and drove my truck with one hand to the dunes around Green Valley. My truck, a shiny silver Nissan 4x4 with black stripes on the side and double tires, was perfect for driving in the desert on such a beautiful day. It was a real man's truck, built to climb hills and stay out of trouble.

Men like me went the dunes every weekend to drive our big trucks and challenge each other on the racetracks that were set up over and around the sand dunes. I was happy steering my truck up and down the dunes. I wanted to forget about Vivian and the day before. I didn't want to think about my boys, hiding behind their grandmother, or about what Vivian had said.

About one thirty in the afternoon, on the edge of the hills, near the main road, I got in a race with a guy I'd seen on the dunes before. He was a Vietnam vet, half Asian and half white, driving a 1992 yellow Toyota pickup. Skinny, all wrinkled and bony, with a close-shaved beard, he always wore a baseball hat pulled low on his bald forehead. He was taller and older than me. I was thirty-three. He was maybe fifty. He had a reputation for being drunk all the time. He probably was drunk when he hit me and drove away.

We started racing, but the guy wasn't following the signals. He drove through a red light, slammed into the side of my truck, and just kept driving. My truck flipped 360 degrees. When it stopped rolling and settled upright, the engine was still running, and the tires weren't flat. I crawled out of the driver's seat, twisting and turning myself out the door until I fell outside on the sand.

"Oh, shit!" The pain was worse than anything I had ever felt before.

I couldn't breathe. I couldn't make a sound. When I heard my truck still running, I forced myself to stand, shake my head, rub my legs, and take a shallow breath. I opened the door, grabbed the steering wheel, and pulled myself back into the truck. I knew I couldn't wait. I had to get to a doctor. Every bump in the road sent pain shooting through my body as I drove fifteen miles to the clinic at Davis–Monthan Air Force Base. I needed help. I had to survive.

Everything hurt—my lungs, stomach, back. There was no blood, but I knew I was hurt bad. It was the beginning of my decent into Hell.

I crawled out of my truck and walked inside the clinic at the army base, trying to look normal. Nobody knew how much I hurt.

"I've been in an accident."

"What kind of an accident?"

"In my truck." I tried to catch my breath. "I am in a lot of pain." I put my hand on my back, low, near my hip.

The nurse called for a cart. "Here, lie down on your stomach. We're going to take you for an X-ray." Three hours later she found me, still back in an exam room.

"Mr. Flores, your back is broken. We can't help you here. This is serious. I'm calling an ambulance. We're sending you to Grand Hospital in Tucson.

The paramedics wheeled me into the ambulance, gave me something strong for the pain and drove me to the door of the emergency room. I answered a few questions and signed a lot of forms I didn't understand.

The clerks asked over and over, "Mr. Flores, is there anyone we should call?"

"No, I'm alone. I don't have anyone."

I don't think I was in my room very long before the doctor walked in. He was younger than me. A good-looking white man with dark black hair, he looked at me with soft brown eyes. He was the same size as me and a very sharp dresser in street clothes. He didn't dress like a doctor, but he had a stethoscope around his neck. His face settled me with his confidence.

"Please, Doctor, I'm a surfer. Just let me step on my board and ride the waves one more time," I begged.

"Ernie, do you remember how this happened?"

"I was in my truck and another truck came over a hill and hit me hard. My truck flipped over on the sand."

I remember every minute of our conversation. We talked for thirty minutes. I told him everything, including that I was a surfer from Mazatlán. I told him that I almost won the Mexican national competition ten years before.

The doctor held the X-rays in his hands and told me that my back was broken in two places. He looked at me and said, "If you do what I tell you, you are going to be okay."

"Will I ever surf again?"

"Yes. But I'm the only one who can do this. It is a new kind of operation. You have to trust me."

"I trust you. Don't let me down."

"No, Ernie. I won't let you down."

We shook hands. He left before he could see me cry. To this day, I remember my doctor's name. I'll never forget it. If I could ever find him again, I would shake his hand and say thank you a million times for what he did. He's the only reason I'm here today.

I spent six days in the hospital. The doctor took bones from my ass to fill in the cracks in my spine. I still have a bar in my back. My tailbone hurts to this day.

On the third day in the hospital, a big male nurse put me into the chlorine bathtub for water therapy. The water was hot. It felt good to sink my body into water again.

After I left the hospital, I went to live with Cachi and his wife in their house in Tucson. I had no job and nowhere else to go. I wore a rigid plastic brace for four months. I didn't take it off except for showering. In December, Cachi and I talked about going back to Mazatlán to see my father.

"It's so damn cold here. Why don't we get on a bus and go back to Mazatlán?" I suggested.

"We should. I want to see the ocean again. I need to get out of here."

The cold hurt my back, and I wanted to see Papí. I wanted him to know I was okay. But first, before getting on the bus, I went to church and took off my brace. I said gracias to the Virgin Mary. I prayed and asked her to take care of me from then on. I left my brace at the altar in front of the church and walked out the door. It was December 12, the Virgin's feast day, exactly four months after my surgery.

My trip to Mazatlán was a blessing and a curse. We were able to see my father alive for just three days. I believe that when Papí saw me and Cachi, all raggedy and half dead from drugs and alcohol, he decided to take the ride to the afterlife for us. We were still here on earth, but he was gone. I was devastated.

My dear, kind, generous, honorable father died of a heart attack on December 15, 1993. I was lost for a long time after he died. He was my protector, my guardian angel. He held me up and never let me down. My father, more than anyone, understood and appreciated me. He taught me it was okay to stand alone. To piss people off. To look different. To be different.

Living in my father's house, even if he was no longer there, I felt his presence every day. I talked to his picture and prayed to the Virgin of Guadalupe, just as he did when I was growing up.

I stayed in Mazatlán for four months before I came back to Tucson in the spring of 1994 to look for the man who caused my accident. I had a big insurance policy, about $300,000 in health insurance to cover my hospital bills, but I couldn't work. I couldn't pay for food or a place to live. I was still getting medical bills that I didn't understand. Every day I remembered the truck and the guy who hit me. He needed to pay for what he did to me.

One day, I saw the *pendejo* driving and chased him to his house. It had been a year since my accident, and he was still driving the same yellow truck. I pounded on his door until he answered.

"Hey. Remember me? I'm the guy you almost killed, racing in the dunes last year."

"Yeah, I remember you. How are you? What do you want?"

"You need to help me out. I need money for living expenses."

I did not realize that my medical bills could be paid by the man's automobile insurance. This man caused the accident. The bills were his responsibility, not mine.

"Come inside. We can talk. Can I get you a beer?"

We drank a lot of beer. I purposely got him drunk because I wanted to hear what he would say.

"I'm sorry for what happened."

"Why didn't you at least stop and see if I was okay?"

"I know I should have, but I was drinking that afternoon. If the police came, I would have been charged with a DUI. I was scared. I went straight home."

He agreed to a write a statement saying that the accident was his fault, but in the end, he didn't sign it. He tricked me. He knew I was from Mexico and I didn't know the laws in the US. In Mexico, almost no one buys insurance, and the transit police don't pay any attention to insurance anyway. I didn't call the police after the accident, and I didn't have a lawyer to tell me what to do. He gave me a useless piece of paper. I was helpless.

Later, the guy called me and said I should come to his house again. "Ernie, I thought about it and I want to do the right thing."

"Okay."

"I don't have any money, but I have three guns I'm ready to give you. They're legal weapons. I can provide the registration papers."

"What am I going to do with three guns?"

"You can sell them for fifteen hundred dollars each. That would be partial payment from me for causing the accident."

"What about the rest?"

"You'll get that from my auto insurance."

"No, *vete al Diablo*. Go to hell! I want you to pay me now."

"Well, I don't have any money now. This is my best offer." He kept saying I had to accept his offer because I was illegal and I had no rights. Finally, I accepted the guns and the registration papers and went home.

Another six months went by. I hired an attorney and went to court. I sued the guy for my lost wages and for pain and suffering. He was found guilty and ordered to pay my costs: $33,000.

I never saw a dime of that money. My attorney told me the man was no longer willing to give me any money for the accident. He got $33,000 from his car insurance, but he wasn't going to give it to me. His lawyer kept half the money, and the man kept the rest of it for himself. My attorney wasn't willing to go any further, and I didn't have money to hire another one. I was out of options.

And to make the whole situation worse, the man went to the police and charged me with breaking into his house and stealing his guns. I was furious. He caused me a lifetime of pain and suffering. He almost kept me from ever surfing again. He stole the money that was coming to me from his insurance company. He lied about giving me three of his guns. And because I wasn't legally in the United States, there wasn't anything I could do about it.

I know I shouldn't have taken the guns. I was not a gun dealer and I wasn't a thief. I immediately regretted my decision to accept the guns, and I regret that decision to this day. I was not thinking clearly. I was young, stupid, confused, alone, and still in a lot of pain. I was so full of rage I didn't care about anyone or anything.

In the end, I sold all but one of the guns. I kept one to shoot him with. For a long time, I wanted to hunt him down and kill him. But my father's words haunted me. "Neto never leave this world with blood on your hands." If the jackass who hit me is still alive, he has *mi padre* to thank.

• • •

I'm happy Papí didn't see how much trouble I got into after he died, but I know he would be proud of the man who I am now. My father was my North Star, guiding my way with his essential good humor and basic decency. When I look to the heavens, he is still there, telling me, "Ernesto, you are a good boy. Make sure that everyone knows that about you."

34
Papí

Sinaloa, Mexico
1917–1993

Perdoname, Papí.
  I miss you every day of my life.
  How I wish you were still here.
  To sing. To make me smile. To make me laugh.
    To make me remember.

Perdoname, Papí.
  You were my Polaris. My guiding light.
  I will never be half the man you were.
  Please forgive me for my sins.

Mi padre, Jesús Flores-Garcia.
  Handsome, proud Mixteco.
  Son of hardworking Maria.
  And gallivanting Juan.

Mi padre, Jesús Flores.
Siempre trajabador.
Mechanic, blacksmith, security guard.
Father. Grandfather. Friend.

Mi padre, Jesús Flores.
Lover of women.
Four sisters, one wife, two daughters, and the
    Virgin Maria.
Never left home before kneeling to pray.

Mi padre, Jesús.
Patient and kind. Tired.
Burned by the sun and the blacksmith fire.
Sang his love for my mother on his way home
    at night, with the tequila bottle in his hand.

Mi padre, Jesús.
Drove his car over a bridge. Sixty-five years old,
    with a gash on his head.
Confused and lost but not yet dead.
A woman found him and took him to her home.
A kind stranger? Or the Virgin Maria?

Mi padre, Jesús.
I found him in Tijuana.
Working in an auto shop, tools in his hands.
Smiled when he saw me.
With tears in our eyes.

Mi padre, Jesús.
Took a bus back home to take care of his family.
No longer lost. Never again drunk.
Only happy to be home. Working. Taking care
of grandchildren.

Mi padre, Jesus,
Heart attack at seventy-five.
Handsome and proud. Patient and kind.
Missed by his wife, his children, his
grandchildren, his neighbors, his friends.
Missed, especially, by me.

Perdoname, Papí.
I miss you every day of my life.
How I wish you were still here.
"Will I ever be half the man you were?"
The answer, loud and clear, is *nunca*. Not ever.

35

Pino

Tucson, Arizona
1997

I arrived in the Tucson bus station at eleven o'clock in the morning with my seventeen-year-old nephew, Lalo. Sitting in the middle section, on the right-hand side of the bus coming from LA, I was going back to Mazatlán with a lot of money and three plastic baggies of cocaine.

I carefully packed the cocaine in my backpack. One large bag, a sixteen-gram stash of coke, a small eight ball of three and a half grams, and another smaller bag, less than two grams, that I was using on the bus. My plan was to use the drugs with Cachi while we were partying with two Indian girls he had just met. I also wanted to sell some in Tucson so I would have extra money in my pocket when I got back to Mazatlán.

Every couple of hours I went to the bathroom to put a pinch of coke in my nose. We weren't allowed to smoke on the bus, and I wanted something to keep me alert. I was eager to be back in Mazatlán. I had spent the past three years working in Las Vegas, doing construction and selling cocaine on the side. I missed being on the water.

I was alone in Vegas most of the time. Thirty-seven years old, with a stab wound in my heart that wouldn't heal. I had no women at night and too much time to think. I missed my boys every minute. I wanted to see my father, to talk to him in person, but he was in a grave in Mazatlán. I had a lot of money and nothing to spend it on except the Black girls who used to come around and offer me a blow job for five dollars. "For ten dollars you can have it all."

Lalo was my favorite nephew, the son of my sister Rosa, who moved back to LA after our father died. I stopped off in LA on my way home from Vegas.

"Lalo, I'm proud of you. You're a smart, clean, hardworking kid. You remind me of myself when I was young, before I started doing all this messy stuff. You're not like your brothers. You'd rather do what is right than make a lot of money."

My plan was to take a bus to Tucson, spend a few days with Cachi, and then go on to Mazatlán.

"Hey, Tio, I'm not doing anything here. Can I come with you? I'd like to see Cachi again. I haven't been to Tucson in a long time."

"Sure. You can come. But be sure you do what I say."

"Of course."

"I'll pay for your ticket. Do you want to come to Mazatlán, too?"

"Maybe. I'll think about it."

If I had known I was going to get in trouble in Tucson, I would have told Lalo to stay home. If I'd taken a plane to Mazatlán, I would have gone right through customs, no questions asked. Every other year I flew, but this year I wanted to say goodbye to Cachi. It was one of the dumbest decisions of my life.

The bus pulled into the station and three policemen came on board—a skinny, old Tucson policeman, a fat Mexican FBI detective, and smart-ass Asian from the DEA. A snitch said that there was someone on the bus with a lot of money. More money than I had. But cops think everyone looks suspicious.

"*Nadie sale de este autobús sin ser buscado,*" Fatso shouted. "Nobody leaves this bus without being searched."

"*Salir del autobús en una sola línea.* Come off the bus in a single line. Bring all your bags with you."

I turned to Lalo and whispered, "Quick. Go ahead of me. Get at least five people ahead of me and don't look back. Never look at me. Go directly to Cachi. He's waiting for us inside the terminal."

I stepped off the bus, trying to look like a tourist with nothing to hide. As soon as I saw dogs with the policeman, I knew this could be serious, but I wasn't worried. I always traveled with a small amount of pepper in a plastic bag in my pocket, as a precaution.

I had been stopped before and never detained. I took a deep breath as I made it past the dogs sniffing my bags of black pepper. I smiled. Again, this time, I made it.

I looked around and saw Cachi and Lalo standing by the fence. The policeman and the FBI agent wanted to talk to me. I told myself to stay calm, but I was sweating in the cold, early February afternoon.

"*Cómo sé llama?*"

"Ernesto Alonso Flores Rodriguez," I answered in English.

"Where is your ID?"

"My driver's license is in my billfold. In my backpack."

"Don't reach for it. We're going to search your backpack. Where did you come from?"

"I was in LA, visiting my sister."

"Why did you come to Tucson?"

"My brother lives here. I want to see him before I go back to Mexico."

I started to relax. I was answering the questions and smiling. I looked them in the eye and didn't look down. I hoped they would forget about my backpack.

This is going to be okay, I thought to myself, until the DEA guy walked over to me. His short black hair was combed straight out from the top of his head. He looked like an angry fighting rooster.

"Put your arms up over your head and take off those sunglasses. Where did you get these expensive sunglasses?" Rooster wanted to know. "I've always wanted a pair of Ray-Bans like that, but I can't afford them."

"My son gave them to me," I said, but I knew I was busted. *Why didn't I just put the sunglasses in my pocket?* I've asked myself that question a hundred times. Having expensive sunglasses, especially ones that guy couldn't afford, made me look guilty.

Rooster patted me all over, and then he searched my backpack. He found the big bag of coke, barely concealed. "Look what I found! Your stash of cocaine. You know what this means, amigo. You are going to jail."

I started talking right away. I told him that it was only for my own use.

"Look, I know I wasn't supposed to have it, okay? But I'm coming here from LA. I always bring my own stash when I'm only staying for a little while, because I don't know if I can find it in a new town."

"Listen, we both know that is bullshit. Get in the white van that's parked over there."

"Where are you taking me?"

"You're going to the 29th Street Jail.

"What about my clothes and stuff?"

"Well, you can't take them with you. You can donate them, or else we'll keep them until someone comes and picks them up for you."

Cachi and Lalo were waiting for me outside the gate. I lifted my chin and did the two-finger peace wave as I climbed into the van going to jail.

It was time to trade my clothes for the navy blue jumpsuit that would be my uniform for the next four months. I wrote a note for Cachi to read when he picked up my things. *Cachi, thank you for keeping these clothes for me until I get out. There is a new pair of blue socks that you can keep. They are a present for you.*

I smiled as I handed the note and the bags to the guard. He never knew that inside the pair of blue socks were the two small bags of cocaine. Together they weighed almost five grams. Cachi was happy with his present.

I spent the first fifteen days in classification, going to hearings and answering questions. I made friends right away. The 29th Street Jail is seven stories tall. I was on the second floor, in a section with eight other guys waiting to go to trial, including Pino, in the next cell.

Pino grew up in Culiacan, about two hundred kilometers from my hometown. We were two *compañeros* from the state of Sinaloa. When we were together, we talked about people we both knew or had heard about. We talked like two people who knew each other for a long time.

Pino had been in the 29th Street Jail for a year. He helped me know the routine those first few weeks. He told me who was mellow and who I should avoid. He warned me when the guards were coming around to spray us.

"Neto, tomorrow the guards are going to spray. Stay mellow. Don't get upset or you will just make trouble for all of us."

The guards sprayed everybody once a month for lice. I remembered what Pino said and stayed cool, even though I wanted to fight all of them when they made me open my fly so they could spray me down there.

One day, Pino showed me how to make tamales that tasted like home, mixing Doritos with boiling water and the packet from a chicken Cup Noodles.

"This is pretty good," I told him. "Not like real tamales but better than Cup Noodles."

Pino was a short, thin guy with a round face. He was so light skinned he was almost white. He had scars on his face and one eye that drooped and blinked when he talked. He was younger than me, but he walked with a limp like an old man. He told me he was a federal agent before joining one of the Sinaloa gangs.

"*De veras?*" I asked Pino one day. "How did you go from being a *federale* to joining the cartel?"

"One day, I was caught in a shoot-out between *federales* and the gang, and I was shot in the neck."

Pino pulled down the collar of his jumpsuit to show me the ugly, deep purple scar near his throat.

"I was almost killed. The *federales* ran away and left me lying in the street."

I nodded my head to keep him talking.

"Two gang members came over and picked me up. I thought they were going to kill me. Instead, one of them stopped the bleeding while another one wrapped my neck in a bandage. The next day they offered me a job."

"Why are you here, Pino? Because you were in a gang?"

"Yes. I think that's the real reason. I was arrested for having a dead body in the trunk of my car."

"Seriously? *Qué pasó?*"

"Well, my car broke down on the road to Hermosillo. The traffic police flashed his lights and pulled over to see why I was stopped. When they opened the trunk, they found the dead guy wrapped in a blanket. Now I'm being charged with kidnapping and murder. But I didn't kill him. And I don't think it is kidnapping if the guy is already dead."

"Why did you have him in the trunk of your car?"

"He was killed by someone I knew. I was just taking him to his brother in Hermosillo so he could have a good resting place in the cemetery. His brother wanted him to be somewhere for his family to visit."

"*Qué lastima.* What is going to happen to you?"

"The district attorney wants me to tell him who killed the guy. I can't do that or I'll be killed next. It's just my bad luck that my car broke down."

One day Pino asked me for a favor. I knew he didn't like his cellmate.

"Neto, there's this big guy in my cell who smells

real bad. He smells like stinky toilet paper. I've got to get him out of my room. He's making me sick."

"What do you want me to do?"

"I need you to push him down the stairs. I can't do it because they will know it was me. You're new here. You don't even know him, so they won't suspect you. If you move real fast, everyone will think it was an accident."

I knew I could do that. The next time I saw the big smelly guy at the top of the stairs, I ran over and gave him a shove. He yelled as he tumbled down the stairs, pushing people out of the way and crashing at the bottom. He never knew who pushed him. It happened so fast I don't think anyone saw me, but if they did, I knew no one would tell.

"What happened?" the guards asked as they ran to see.

"I don't know," said the big smelly guy. "I guess I tripped."

The guy wasn't hurt seriously. Just a bad twist on his ankle. He went to the nurse's station and never went back to Pino's cell again.

"Thanks, Neto,. Pino said the next day. "I'll take care of you for as long as you are here."

Pino continued to live next door to me. Every week, for as long as I was in the 29th Street Jail, he sent me a Cup Noodles and a small bag of Doritos. Sometimes he even bought me a cup of coffee.

36

The Artist

My life was in shambles. I lost my way in a life of drugs and crime. My soul was tangled with bad decisions. I was rich but I wasn't happy. And then Fate put me back in jail again. I'd been here many times. I'm ok in detention. Next to the ocean, it is my second home. I stay out of trouble and make friends with the guards. They do their job. I do mine. The only difference is they go home to their families at night and I am locked in a cell surrounded by concrete and other men too poor to buy their way out.

I stayed on the second floor of the 29th Street Jail with prisoners waiting to be classified. After two weeks, my first cellmate moved. I never knew why. The next day I had a new cellmate, Issi Martinez, a quiet man with the same name as my friend from the military school when I was five. Younger than me, Issi was only twenty-four years old. Half Mexican and half Acoma Indian, Issi was tall and strong. His thick, black hair hung straight down his back. He'd already spent two years in jail, fighting for his freedom.

"Why are you here?" Issi lowered his voice to a whisper and leaned toward me.

"I was caught with cocaine, coming off the bus from LA to Tucson. What about you?"

"I was spray-painting a mural under the bridge outside of Tucson."

"What kind of mural?"

"It was mural about Mexicans and Indians from years ago. I worked on it for a long time. I was practically finished with it when my life almost came to an end."

He coughed and cleared his throat with a swallow. "I heard someone sneak up behind me. The guy put a gun to the back of my head. I heard the trigger click. I knew he was going to kill me."

"Yeah?"

"I didn't have any weapons on me, just the paint can that was in my hand. I swung around and hit the guy in the mouth with the can, as hard as I could."

"Wasn't it self-defense?"

"Yeah, it was self-defense. But the guy was a cop. I knocked out two of his teeth with the paint can. Now I'm charged with assaulting a police officer. They are trying to make it attempted murder."

"Did you know he was a cop?"

"No. He never said he was. He never told me to drop the paint can. I still think he would have killed me if I didn't knock out his teeth."

Me and Issi became good friends. Just like I was with my other Issi friend, thirty-two years before. We watched out for each other and stayed out of trouble. We didn't jump anybody, and nobody jumped us. Even though we were in minimum security, there were a lot of fights almost every day. Blacks against Mexicans. Bloods against Crips. Mexicans against Whites.

Issi taught me to be silent and watch everything that happened. Neither one of us wanted to fight. Instead, we stayed in our cell a lot. I read books, and Issi drew pictures and wrote poems in his notebooks.

Issi grew up in Tucson. He was the first person in his family who graduated from high school. He started drawing street murals when he was fourteen, about the same age I was when I started surfing. He liked to make murals that told stories. He dreamed of being a famous mural artist just like I dreamed of becoming a champion surfer. Now here we were, locked up together in a fortress of broken dreams.

I loved Issi's drawings and his beautiful handwriting. He could draw anything. People, scenery, and sea creatures. All kinds of animals. Horses, rabbits, dogs, and donkeys. He drew everyday people and ancient heroes. He didn't need to look at anything. He saw things in his mind that other people couldn't see—

poems, sensitive words, beautiful pictures. He imagined the picture in his head and drew it on paper.

One day I woke up with an idea. "Hey, Issi, can you make me a card to send to my sister?"

"Sure. What do you want?"

"Something she would like to see."

"I could draw a picture of you looking out a window, wanting to see her again."

"That's exactly what I want. Can you make the person really look like me?"

"I can do that. Do you want me to put some words inside?"

"Maybe write a poem about how much I miss her. And wish her a happy *Día de Amor y Amistad.*"

Valentine's Day had just passed, but it was too early for Easter. I knew Alicia would appreciate hearing from me. She had always been a good sister. I wanted her to know that I missed her and that I was thinking of her.

Issi's card was perfect. The picture of me with my long curly hair, wearing a prison jumpsuit, looked just like me. He drew flowers and hearts on the outside of the envelope. His writing inside the card was as beautiful as the pictures on the outside. *Dear Alicia, I look at the moon from this tiny window and think of you looking at the same moon from your home in LA. The moon smiles on both of us until I see you again. Amor para siempre. Tu hermano, Neto.*

That night, before I sent the card to my sister, I

showed it to the other inmates in the cafeteria. Even the guards were amazed. Soon, I was promoting Issi's cards wherever I went.

"Neto, can you ask Issi to make a card for me?"

"Of course. But it will cost you three dollars. Who is this card for?"

Issi made cards for girlfriends and for mothers. For sons and daughters, nieces and nephews. He drew hilarious cartoons and wrote beautiful love poems. We had a good business together. And it was all perfectly legal.

37

The Judge

The guards led me through the big wooden doors of the courtroom. I'd been here before.

The judge leaned forward, resting his elbows on the front of his desk. The courtroom was full of people waiting for him to make decisions. Decisions that could change their lives. We were all hoping for the best but afraid that, instead, we would be locked up for a long time. We all knew we were guilty.

I waited and listened to other cases until it was my turn. This was not the first time I'd been here. I knew where to sit and how to behave. *Sit quietly. Don't fidget. Don't look around at the other inmates. Slump my shoulders and look down. Look humble. This will be over soon.*

The clerk called my name. I walked to the front of the room, to the witness stand, and nodded briefly at the judge. *What is it about this time that makes my legs feel weak? That makes my stomach hurt?*

Judge's eyes were tired as he looked up at me from the file in his hand. He shook his head from side to side. I knew he recognized me. I held on to the stand in front of me, to keep my cold hands steady. I didn't want him to see me in his courtroom, wearing a blue jumpsuit. I didn't want him to know that I was arrested for drugs again. I had to get control of myself.

Judge pressed his lips together before he spoke. His voice was calm and steady. "You're not the same Ernesto Flores who I met in this very courtroom two years ago, are you?"

"Yes, sir. That's me."

He rubbed his hand through his thick black hair. "But Mr. Flores, you were doing well. What happened to you?"

"I'm sorry, Judge. Three days ago, I was stopped by federal agents when I was coming off the bus from Los Angeles. I had cocaine on me."

"And why was that, Mr. Flores?

"I was going to use it while I was in Tucson. It was only for my personal use, sir."

"Mr. Flores, it says here that you had a large bag of cocaine weighing more than sixteen grams when you were searched. That is a lot of cocaine. I have a very hard time believing that you were going to use all that by yourself."

"Well, Judge, I thought I might share it with some people if I got invited to a party."

People behind me in the courtroom started to

laugh quietly. I didn't turn around, but I could hear them whispering to each other. Judge opened his eyes wide and smacked his hammer on the top of his desk.

"That's enough, Mr. Flores. I'm sending you to back to county jail until we decide what to do with you. Please don't get in any trouble while you are here. I'll see you back in this courtroom in a month."

"Thank you very much, sir. I will be good."

• • •

I met Judge Anderson for the first time two years before, in 1995. He was about sixty years old, and I was thirty-five. I had just broken up with my girlfriend, Yolanda, and I was on a rampage for leaving her. I was out making a scene, and one of the neighbors yelled that some drugs were missing. Some *cabron* called the police, and they noticed that I had needle tracks on my arm. I was busted for using drugs and for causing a disturbance.

I noticed right away that Judge Anderson was not a usual judge. He was kind and thoughtful, taking his time before making a decision. A short, well-built Black man, his hair was trimmed close to his head. His shiny eyes were as black as his robe.

"Why do you have those needle marks on your arm, Mr. Flores?"

"They are from heroin, sir. I was using it with my girlfriend. I got used to it and couldn't quit."

"Do you think you can quit now, Mr. Flores?

"I guess I have to, sir."

Judge Anderson looked straight at me. "I need to decide what to do with you, Mr. Flores. I can see that you are polite and respectful. I like the fact that you told me the truth. I think maybe I can help you."

Judge explained that there was a government program in Tucson for drug users like me. "I want you to stop using drugs, Mr. Flores, and get your high school diploma. How does that sound?"

"I would like that, sir."

"Okay. I'm going to give you six months to get your GED. I want you to work hard in school every morning and go to a job in the afternoons. You don't have to go to jail while you are in school, but I want you to get cleaned up. Do you have a job now?"

"Yes, sir, I help my friend Teddy in his auto shop. We work on undercover cop cars."

"Well, keep working. Stop using drugs. Go to school. Come back to my courtroom with your GED certificate and these charges will be dropped. Do you think you can do that?"

"I know I can."

And that's what I did. Every day Teddy drove me to the GED school and dropped me off. Then he went to the titty bars until noon, when it was time to pick me up, and we'd go back to work.

My teachers, Rosie and Maria, worked hard with me and the rest of the students in the government school. They were about forty years old—a few years older than me. Our teachers spoke to us in Spanish and in English. I liked them a lot. They were both pretty and cute with long black hair, dark eyes, and kissable red lips. They worried about us. They didn't want us to go back to jail.

The classroom was in a warehouse building in the center of a big, gated parking lot. Once we were checked in, we couldn't leave the parking lot. There were no windows in the school to look out of, but there was air conditioning so we wouldn't get too hot. The classroom door was closed, and school started at nine. Every hour we had a break, so we could go out to the parking lot to talk and smoke cigarettes.

All of the students were from detention places. Rosie and Maria separated the class into men and women. They took turns with each group. There were only three men in the class—me, one Black guy, and one Indian. We sat in a circle with the teacher in the center. The teacher wrote down questions for us to answer. Questions about history and presidents, geography, and English. We did a lot of writing and had conversations. We wrote essays and read them out loud to each other. We practiced spelling and took tests. The subjects were easy for me, and I liked being in school again. There were mostly pregnant teenage girls in that school, but I was the only student who showed up every single day.

Four and a half months later, I was back in Judge

Anderson's courtroom, clean and sober, with my GED certificate in my hand.

"Well done, Mr. Flores. You got your GED in less than six months."

"Well, I went every day, sir."

"I'm going to dismiss these charges, but please try to stay out of trouble. I believe in you or I wouldn't have given you this chance."

"Thank you again, sir." I wanted to shake Judge's hand, but I knew I shouldn't do that. I gave him a big smile instead and said thank you with my eyes.

• • •

Now, here I was again, back in Judge Anderson's courtroom, this time in a navy-blue jumpsuit. I was arrested for possession of cocaine on February 3, 1997. On March 3, I was back in Judge Anderson's courtroom.

The judge met with the prosecutor and my public defender before calling me up. They talked for what seemed like a long time.

"Do you swear to tell the truth, the whole truth, and nothing but the truth, so help you God?"

"Yes, sir. I do."

I needed to spit but had to swallow instead. I could feel my face tingling with embarrassment. I knew I wasn't charming or cool. I was stupid. A guy who didn't learn from his mistakes.

The judge looked at me hard and shook his head. "Okay, Mr. Flores, here is what I can offer you. You can stay where you are, in county jail, or plead guilty to possession of drugs, which is a felony, and spend two years in a federal prison."

"That doesn't sound too good, sir. I think I will stay in county jail and see if you can come up with something better for me next time."

"Thank you, Mr. Flores. I'll see you back here in one month."

Issi was happy to see me when I came back in handcuffs. We'd become friends and business partners. We made our own hand weights, filling plastic bags with water, and exercised alone in our cell. We socialized with other inmates when we had to, but mostly we stayed out of the way. Issi kept me calm.

One month later, in April, I said goodbye to Issi, not knowing what was going to happen in court. Again there was a meeting with Judge Anderson, the district attorney, and my public defender, who didn't seem to recognize me.

They finished talking. Judge Anderson cleared his throat and asked, "How are you, Mr. Flores?"

"I am well, sir. How are you?"

"I am tired. This month I have another offer for you. I can reduce your sentence by six months. Stay in county jail or spend a year and a half in federal prison."

"I think I will stay in county jail, sir. I really don't want to go to federal prison."

I walked back into my cell. Issi shook my hand and patted my shoulder. I looked forward to more conversations. We talked about our life before jail and the criminal injustice system. We knew that we were locked up, in part, because we grew up poor and our skin was dark. People in Tucson, walking past Issi's murals, stopped and took pictures. They smiled and said they wished they had that much talent. They had no idea that the artist was in the 29th Street Jail.

I knew I shouldn't have been using and selling drugs. But I also knew that a lot of my customers were rich businessmen and housewives who wanted to party with cocaine, same as me. But I was in jail and they never would be.

Issi's mother and sister lived in a trailer court across the street from the jail, but they never came to visit him, not even once. He talked about them a lot. I wondered if he would ever see them again.

Issi didn't use drugs at all. He never had. Not even weed.

"Neto, why do you use drugs? I never understood why people think they need to do that."

"I started out smoking weed with my friends when I was first learning to surf. I liked it a lot. All the surfers were doing it. It made me feel powerful and relaxed at the same time."

"Did you ever not smoke weed?"

"When my sons were born, I gave it up. My wife didn't like it. I wanted to be a good father, so I quit."

"And then what happened to you?"

"I kept using weed on the sly when I started arguing with my wife."

"I mean, why did you start using bigger stuff again?"

"My life fell apart. I was living in Tucson and Las Vegas. I was in the desert with no water anywhere. My wife left me. I broke my back in an accident in the sand dunes. I didn't see my kids anymore. My father died. I missed the ocean. I was lonely and I didn't recognize myself. Heroin and cocaine were right there, next to me. I should have died. A lot of people did. But I kept getting arrested, and every time I went to jail, I was able to start over."

"Was it hard?"

"Not really. Quitting heroin was hard. Cocaine was pretty easy. Two years ago, when the judge gave me a second chance, I got clean. I wanted to stay that way."

"And?"

"I went back to Vegas and started working construction again for a friend. I was working nights and trying to sleep during the day. Pretty soon I was dealing drugs again and making a lot of money. But my life was empty. I missed my father. I missed my boys. I missed Darnell. I even missed Ruco. I missed the person I used to be."

"Why didn't you stay in Tucson?"

"I should have. I wish I had. I really didn't know what to do."

Soon it was May—time for another court appearance. Another goodbye. As I walked out of our cell, Issi whispered, "Be careful, amigo. They are going to keep throwing stuff at you. Some things they will have dug up from years ago. Some things they will just make up and throw at you, even if they aren't true."

This time, Judge Richardson said, "Mr. Flores, it has come to my attention that this will be your third felony conviction."

"No, sir, that's not right. I've never been convicted of a felony. I've been arrested and gone to jail a lot, but only for misdemeanors. I've done a lot of stupid things, but I've never killed a person or committed a felony."

"Okay, here's my offer. How about a year in federal prison? Or do you want to go back to county jail?"

"If I go to federal prison, do I need to say I committed a felony?"

"Yes, Ernesto. You know that's how it works."

"Thank you very much, Judge. But I think I'll stay right here."

• • •

At the end of May, Izzi started saying goodbye for good.

"Neto, there isn't much more they can offer you. They're going to send you back to Mexico."

Another day in court. The prosecutor smiled as he handed the judge a piece of paper. Judge Anderson rubbed his hand on the back of his neck. He loosened the collar of his shirt. His black robe wrinkled as he looked at the piece of paper in front of him. He called my name. I stood up next to my public defender.

"Mr. Flores, this report says that you are in the United States illegally. Is that true?"

"Yes, sir, that's true."

"How long have you been coming to the US?"

"Since I was fourteen, sir. I crossed the border by myself because I wanted to learn English."

Before I knew it, I was telling Judge Anderson my whole life story. It felt like me and the judge and the lady who was typing were the only people in the room.

"I was going to school and learning a lot when cops with police dogs came into my class and arrested me. They said I was part of a fight, but I wasn't. I wasn't even at school when the fight happened."

Judge Anderson listened carefully as I told him my whole story. He didn't interrupt me. He let me talk until I was finished telling him everything.

"I'm sorry that happened to you, Mr. Flores. It sounds like you were on a good path when you were fourteen."

"Yes, sir. I was. I came to the US to learn English and not to do anything bad."

"How many times did you come back into the US without papers?"

"I came back when I was twenty-two and spent

most of the past fifteen years here. But I liked to go back to Mazatlán for a visit every two years."

"Well, I think it is time for you to go back to Mexico and stay there. What do you think?"

"Well, actually, sir, that's where I was going when I was busted coming off the bus. I was going to make a quick stop to say goodbye to some people and then go back to Mazatlán."

"Here is what I can offer you now, Mr. Flores. I am sending you to the Federal Immigration Detention Center here in Tucson. You can volunteer to be deported. If you volunteer, you will be on a bus to Mexico in three days. If you decide to stay in the immigration prison and fight for your right to be in this country, it will take you a long time to see a judge. It might be five years. Frankly, with your record, you don't have much of a defense."

I knew that this would be my last time to see Judge Anderson. I knew that in a strange way, I would miss him. He reminded me of my father and of my uncles in La Hacienda. He believed in me, and I messed up. I disappointed myself. I probably disappointed him, too.

"I'm okay with going back to Mazatlán, sir. I need to be near the water. Five years in immigration detention is a long time for me to be away from the ocean."

"I understand. So, go home, stay in Mexico for ten years, and then you can apply to come back to the US legally. Do you understand? No more jumping the border every time you feel like it."

"Yes, sir. I understand. If I return to Mexico now, I don't plead guilty to a felony and I don't go to federal prison. My record is clean."

"That's right. And one more thing, Mr. Flores. Listen carefully."

"I'm listening, sir."

"This is your third drug-related offense. I believe you have a serious problem. I want you to use your time in Mexico to do whatever is necessary to stop using. Go into treatment. Find a group to join. Stay away from other drug users. Learn to say no. Can you do that?"

"Yes, sir. I will. I promise you that I will."

The guards led me out of Judge Anderson's courtroom, and I never saw him or my friend Issi again. I was promptly processed out of the 29th Street Jail and put in a van to the federal immigration detention center.

I called Cachi, who came to see me and say goodbye. He brought me fifty dollars from my sister Alicia.

I leaned back in my seat and smiled. I was on my way home.

EPILOGUE

. . .

Epilogue

Sinners and Saints. I was both. I spent twenty years between Heaven and Hell. My life was a hurricane. Swirling out of control and destroying everything in its path.

During the twenty years I spent in the United States, I disappointed everyone who cared about me. Everyone I loved. I disappointed my father, the best employer I ever had, and lovers who gave me more chances than I deserved. I was in trouble with the police, slept with too many women, and went to jail more times than I can count. Most importantly, I abandoned people I loved when I was ordered to leave the United States.

Sinners were all around me. Gangsters. Drug dealers. Members of the Mexican Mafia. I came close to being shot, and I almost killed a man because my Mexican pride was hurt. I lost my way. I fought with the devil and I lost my soul.

And yet, most of time, I struggled to find my way back. I listened to my father's voice. I often tried to stop using drugs, but I fell down the same black hole again, back to my raggedy ways, until I was thrown back in jail and eventually out of the United States.

I wrote this book because I have a story to tell. A message that good people can do bad things. And that bad people can change. Redemption is possible. I jumped from being confined to being free and back again. I prefer being free, but I learned more and became a better person during the times I was confined. There are angels who guide us if we listen to them. And listen to them, we must.

I grew up energetic and curious, always on the lookout for the next adventure. Some things came easy for me. I was good in school, on the soccer field, and in the ocean. I made friends with strangers and found my way in foreign cities. I learned to cook, to work on a shrimp boat and on a printing press, and to speak English as well as Spanish.

I am proud of the times I helped my fellow citizens: helping poor people cross into the United States, saving people from drowning, making people laugh during hard times, and being loyal to my friends. Remembering those years makes me smile.

I want to ask for forgiveness for the times I cheated and lied. Times when I was more violent than I should have been. Times when I broke my promises and destroyed everything. For all those years, I am deeply sorry.

I lost track of all but a few people I knew in the United States. I regret that. For the most part, they were good people. They believed in me and helped me become the man I am today. I wish them good health, dear friends, and memories enjoyable enough to last a lifetime.

After being told by Judge Anderson that it was time for me to go home, that's what I did. I went back to my house on Papagayo Street in Mazatlán. I was thirty-seven years old and eager to be back in the ocean. I was a surfer. A good neighbor. A mother's son.

Finding my way in the ocean was easy. Finding my way on land was not. I promised the judge I would stop using drugs, but temptation was everywhere. I needed an honest job. I needed people to help me. I joined Narcotics Anonymous, found a sponsor, and stayed away from marijuana and hard drugs. I eventually quit alcohol, too.

I fathered two daughters by a woman I call Loca. Although I never loved Loca, I loved my girls just as I loved my boys, twenty years before. I walked the girls to school every day and lived with them until 2005, when Loca kicked me out. For the next nine months, I stayed by the ocean, sleeping in the sand, and taking free showers along the beach.

I tried to reestablish a relationship with my brothers and sisters. Sometimes that worked. Mostly it didn't. I hadn't been home long when I met a guy named Publio in front of the OXXO by my home. Publio was big guy, with long dreadlocks, a quick smile, and a quiet voice. I asked him if he liked the music of Bob Marley. He told me that he was a drummer in a reggae band and had just come back from Mexico City.

I asked Publio if he was a surfer. He said he tried when he was younger, but he'd like to get better. Publio's mother never forgave me for leading him astray. But we weren't astray. We were good friends, focused on surfing and taking care of our families. We were each other's right-hand man whenever a job needed a right hand. He is my brother, the brother I was looking for all my life.

I worked a variety of jobs—guarding a parking lot and selling tours and *mariscos* to tourists along the beach. In 2005, I met a sad-faced American woman sitting on a bench in front of Olas Altas Beach. She told me she had just bought a big house and didn't have anyone to help her take care of it. She invited me to take a look and hired me as her handyman, and we've been friends ever since.

I remodeled Lynda's big home into a place for tourists to stay. People came from all over the world. Students from Australian and Finland came to study

Spanish. Travelers from Canada came to spend winters in a warm place. Some, like Eunice and Gordon, came every year from Saskatchewan and became my dear friends. Some of the other colorful tourists stayed for just one season and were a handful. Remembering all of them makes me smile.

Lynda sold the house in 2010 and moved back to Denver. I went to live with my mother in the house on Papagayo Street.

I applied for a tourist visa to the US. I had been away for more than ten years, and I was eligible to enter the country legally. I had a passport, a portfolio of documents, and all the letters I needed for a visa, but I was "permanently denied," according to a jackass at the US Customs office. He said that all of my wrongdoings were on record, including the report that I killed Cookie, the dog, by rolling over on him in my sleep. I argued that I had never been convicted of a felony, but Mr. Jackass told me that I had enough misdemeanors to keep me out. He said I was a "bad person, not the kind of person we want in the United States."

"You are not the kind of person we want in Mexico either," I told him. "But I guess we're stuck with you."

A lot of people in these stories are gone. All of my uncles are gone, except for Uncle Mon, who still rides horses in the local rodeo and often rides his mule to rescue animals in distress. Uncle Gero died last year at the age of ninety-five. Aunt Valvina is alive and spends most of her time with her sons and daughters in Los Angeles.

So many died young. Cachi was killed in an auto accident in 2002. My brother Pablo died last year after a short illness. Alicia's husband and her son died within a few years of each other. I know I am lucky to be alive.

And what about the other original members of the Olas Altas Crew? *Mis amigos del mar?* Thanks to Facebook, I am in touch with Paco, who lives with his wife and three stepdaughters in Denver. The rest of the crew, however, are no longer in my life.

Donato, our leader and big brother, died in California last year of a brain tumor. Lobo gave up surfing and wandered the streets of Mazatlán for years, still handsome, always drunk. Last year he stumbled on the sidewalk, hit his head on the concrete, and died instantly.

Checo, my friend and main competitor, the one who held the most promise of all of us, was killed by a Mazatlán policeman in 1996. According to people who were there, Checo was high on inhalants. He charged a policeman, threatening to stab him with an ice pick. The policeman didn't hesitate. He pulled out his gun and shot him.

Nolas, my original best friend and first surfing buddy, spent seven years in a Mexican prison for being in possession of seven kilos of marijuana. He was set up by people he trusted from our old neighborhood. Nolas came out of prison in 1988, a bitter, angry man, and he left for California the next day. Although Nolas is no longer part of my life, I hope that he still goes to the ocean from time to time and that when he does, he thinks of me.

I am the only one of the Olas Altas Crew who still surfs regularly. I compete when I can. I am now in the category of "old men," and I often take home prizes, just as I did when I was young. As one of the few surfing pioneers who still surfs regularly, I am something of a celebrity in the Mexican surfing community. Young surfers ask me to tell them stories about the old days. They call me Ruko and want to shake my hand. They tell me I am the godfather of surfing in Mazatlán.

I've been a rich man in America, and now I am a poor man in Mexico. But I'm not running from anything. I love what I do every day and stay committed to my passion—the ocean. My greatest joys are jumping on my board and riding the waves during the day and then sitting back to watch the sunset as the sun disappears with a splash into the ocean.

Although now destined to live in Mexico, I still consider myself a citizen of the world, worthy of the sweet life I live and yet always interested in what more is out there. I have long conversations with tourists from around the world. I study other places and dream of someday visiting exotic lands. But my world is the ocean. It is where I belong.

Like the ocean, there are changes in my life every day and yet my spirit remains the same. Like the ocean, I feel powerful and calm at the same time. I focus on what is good and try to stay away from what isn't. I start every day with a smile.

What matters most is not what I have now, but what I leave behind. A mind that is alive and interested. A heart full of love. A soul worthy of the life I want to live. A man worthy of my father's good name.

Reader's Guide

1. Ernesto was sent to military school at the age of five. How did the experience of being away from home for four years impact the rest of Neto's life? Was it a good decision for his parents to send him away? Did the experience damage him or improve his life?

2. Ernesto's relationships with his parents shaped his life from a very early age. What are your impressions of his mother, Zelmira Rodriguez, and his father, Jesús Flores?

3. Religion is important in Mexican culture, especially a belief in angels and a devotion to the Virgin of Guadalupe. Ernesto's father believes that the Virgin Mary saved him from dying after his automobile accident. Can you relate to his faith in things he can't know for sure?

4. Neto was unjustly accused of being in a fight at his American high school, arrested, and immediately deported. What effect did this have on Ernesto later in his life? How do you think his life might have been different if that had not happened to him?

5. Discuss Ernesto's sexual experience with Juana, Luci's mother. Was it important for Juana to teach Ernesto this lesson in order to protect her daughter? Or were her actions sexual abuse? How did the experience later color Neto's attitudes toward sex?

6. Neto has a deep connection to the ocean. It brings him joy. How does it help him find meaning and purpose in his life? Do you share Neto's deep connection to a thing or place?

7. Ernesto is a handsome man, with an abundance of sexual energy and Mexican charm. He has "a way with the ladies" that sometimes makes him irresistible. How was this both a blessing and a curse in his life?

8. Ernesto is able to look back on his life and recognize that circumstances have not been kind to him and yet remain accountable for his actions. Can you give an example of this?

9. Neto says, "Redemption is always possible if we listen to our better angels. And listen to them, we must." Neto was a coyote, a drug dealer, and a philanderer. Can someone be a good person and still doing bad things? Do you agree that redemption is always possible?

10. Although Neto thinks of himself as a citizen of the world, he is always happy to be home. Talk about what home means to Neto. What does home mean to you?

Acknowledgments

From Lynda:

First and foremost, thank you, Neto, for trusting me to tell your story. The day I met you on the beach was one of the very best days of my life. I could not have moved to Mazatlán without you. You helped me settle into my new home. Not only did you do painting, plumbing and install a beautiful fountain, but you let me see Mazatlán through your eyes. From your stories, I learned to love the city and the people as you do. Your delightful sense of humor, your ability to laugh in the face of adversity, and your wonderful, kind spirit will forever be woven into the fabric of my life.

I know that every one of us has a purpose and a destiny to fulfill while we are here on earth. I know that no matter how far this journey takes you, Neto, your corner of the world will be a better place because you are there.

There are many kinds of heroes in this world. There are important people who risk their lives to save others. But more important, to my mind, are the people who tell the truth—to the world and to themselves—

because the risk is greater, and the applause is often never there. Neto, you will always be my hero.

I also want to thank Victoria Griffin of Blue Pen publishing services, without whom this book would never have been finished. Victoria, your brilliant insights helped me tell Neto's story as I wanted it to be told. Thank you for your unwavering encouragement and support.

And to my family and friends, thank you as well. When I told you I wanted to move to Mexico, you told me to follow my dream. When I told you I wanted to write a book, you believed that I could. You've cheered me on, every step of the way. I couldn't have gone on this journey without you. You are forever in my heart.

About the Authors

Ernesto (Neto) Flores

Ernesto (Neto) Flores is a father, a son, a brother, and a friend. But most of all, he is a surfer.

A native of Mazatlán, México, Neto was part of the Olas Altas Crew, a pack of teenage boys who were Mazatlán's early surfing pioneers in the 1970s. Outgoing and athletic, Neto loves the ocean and all the creatures that call it home.

In his next life, Neto would like to be a giant sea turtle, quietly swimming the waters of the Pacific. For now, he's content to go to the ocean every day, to ride his board when the waves are high, to swim when the ocean is quiet, and to sit along the shore, watching the sunset at the end of each day.

Lynda Jones

Lynda Jones worked as a social worker in the Denver area for more than thirty years. After retiring, she wanted to do something different. Something she'd never done before. She moved to Mazatlán, bought an historic hacienda, remodeled it, and spent five years running a guest home for travelers from around the world.

Lynda met Ernesto Flores, the inspiration for *Citizen of the World*, while sitting on a bench on Olas Altas Beach. Ernesto was selling tours and seafood. Lynda told him she didn't need any seafood or a tour, but she did need a handyman to build a fountain for her courtyard. Ernesto volunteered, and they have been friends ever since.

Lynda's writing reflects her love for the Mexican people and their culture. Although she has moved back to Colorado, she travels to Mexico frequently. Her favorite parts of traveling are the stories she hears along the way.

Visit Lynda's website at www.lyndajoneswriter.com.

lynda@lyndajoneswriter.com
Facebook.com/lyndajoneswriter
Pinterest.com/sirenagrandma
LinkedIn.com/in/lynda-jones-b661b247
Goodreads.com/user/show/1759636-lynda-jones

Made in the USA
Columbia, SC
11 March 2023

13547529R00193